Little Women

A Comedy in Four Acts

Marian De Forest

Adapted from the Story by
Louise M. Alcott

By Arrangement with
Jessie Bonstelle

A SAMUEL FRENCH ACTING EDITION

SAMUEL FRENCH

FOUNDED 1830

SAMUELFRENCH.COM
SAMUELFRENCH-LONDON.CO.UK

CHARACTERS IN THE PLAY

Mr. March
Mrs. March
Meg
Jo
Beth
Amy
Aunt March
Mr. Laurence
Laurie
Professor Bhaer
John Brooke
Hannah Mullett

SYNOPSIS

ACT I—Sitting room of the March home in Concord, Mass., December, 1863.

"It was a comfortable old place, though the carpet was faded and the furniture very plain, for a good picture or two hung on the walls, books filled the recesses, chrysanthemums and Christmas roses blossomed in the windows, and a pleasant atmosphere of home peace pervaded it."

ACT II.—Scene I.—The same, three months later. Morning, March, 1864.

(The curtain will be lowered for a few moments to denote a lapse of time.)

Scene II.—The same, six months later. Late afternoon, September, 1864.

ACT III.—The same, two and one-half years later. Afternoon.

ACT IV.—The apple orchard, Plumfield, eighteen months later. Afternoon, October, 1868.

———

The play staged in New York by Jessie Bonstelle and Bertram Harrison. In London, England, by Jessie Bonstelle.

LITTLE WOMEN

Original cast as produced in New York City at The Playhouse, October, 1912, by William A. Brady.

MR. MARCH	*Lynn Hammond*
MRS. MARCH	*Gertrude Berkeley*
MEG	*Alice Brady*
JO	*Marie Pavey*
BETH	*Gladys Hulette*
AMY	*Beverly West*
AUNT MARCH	*Mrs. E. A. Eberle*
MR. LAURENCE	*Carson Davenport*
LAURIE	*Howard Estabrook*
PROFESSOR FREDERICH BHAER	*Carl Sauerman*
JOHN BROOKE	*John Cromwell*
HANNAH MULLETT	*Lillian Dix*

Original cast for the London production, New Theatre, November 10, 1919.

MR. MARCH	*Alfred A. Harris*
MRS. MARCH	*Henrietta Watson*
MEG	*Joyce Carey*
JO	*Katharine Cornell*
BETH	*Hattie Hanson*
AMY	*Eva Rowland*
AUNT MARCH	*Kate Phillips*
MR. LAURENCE	*Sydney Paxton*
LAURIE	*Antony Holles*
PROFESSOR ANTOINE BARET	*Leslie Faber*
JOHN BROOKE	*Henry C. Hewitt*
HANNAH MULLETT	*Ada Palmer*

NOTE.—For the English production the character of PROFESSOR BHAER, which is German, was changed to that of Professor Antoine Baret, and the speeches were rewritten into French.

NOTE

For the rehearsal in the first act, the text is taken almost verbatim from "Comic Tragedies by Jo and Meg," the book published by Little, Brown & Co., of Boston, Mass., U.S.A., of the plays written by Jo and Meg and acted by the Little Women. The names of the characters are from "Norma, or the Witch's Curse," and "The Captive of Castile, or the Moorish Maiden's Vow."

Little Women

ACT I

SCENE.—*Sitting room in the March home.*
"It was a comfortable old place, though the carpet was faded and the furniture very plain, for a good picture or two hung on the walls; books filled the recesses, chrysanthemums and Christmas roses blossomed in the windows, and a pleasant atmosphere of home peace pervaded it."

TIME.—*Afternoon, December,* 1863.

SETTING.—*Set for Act I, also for Acts II and III, which are not changed, except for the back drops, which are changed for the season of the year.*
Large, square, old-fashioned sitting room, with deep wide window at centre back, filled with growing plants. The window is backed by drop, showing LAURENCE *mansion across the garden. Scene stands for three acts, only the drop changed.*
The March room, with plain white ceiling— scene not over 16 *feet in height, old-fashioned wall paper, with border and baseboard. Niche in the wall on right side of window at back.*

7

A little cupboard underneath it where MEG *gets* BETH'S *picturebook. Both side walls oblique toward the back. Hall door in flat left 1st, showing little trellis and porch and crude wooden seat; window, left 2d. From left 3d, old-fashioned staircase runs back and up about six steps to a square landing, then three steps to platform off into an arched exit left 3. Old-fashioned small oval window in flat on top of staircase. Coat closet under staircase and seat in the elbow of staircase. Mahogany newel posts, white spindles. Mahogany handrail, very solid.*

Right, 1st, door leading into MR. MARCH'S *study, in wing. Right 2d, old-fashioned fireplace and mantel, with brass andirons, logs, bellows, poker, hearth-brush, etc., everything for practical use. On mantel, brass candlesticks, clock, Parian figure of Venus. Right 3d, double doors to dining room. Backing set oblique so as to show suggestion of dining room. Lace-curtained windows in backing.*

Furniture, old mahogany and rosewood, covered with haircloth or faded tapestry or damask. Faded Brussels carpet of old-fashioned, flowered pattern. Rug in front of fireplace Large easy chair R. *Footstool* R. *Round mahogany table with one centre leg* C. *Large upholstered chair* R. *of table. Small chair back of table. Old-fashioned Windsor chair with cretonne seat and back cushions tied on* L. *of table. Old-fashioned sofa with pillows placed in window in Act 3d. Smaller chairs; work-baskets. Whatnot in corner; bust of Plato in niche at back. Bust of Shakespeare on hanging bookshelves on wall at back. Bust of Mozart on piano, which is an old-fashioned cottage upright with candlesticks. This sets against right side of staircase, forming space for three-cornered whatnot.*

NOTE.—*The study door right 1st—solid mahogany (painted white china knobs on all doors)—opens up and off-stage. Double mahogany doors open off into dining room. Door under staircase to closet white like woodwork, with large black hinges. Door left 1st, mahogany. Open on stage and up—brass knocker on the outside.*

LIGHTS.—*At rise LIGHTS AMBER.*

NOTE.—*No change of lights was made during first act in New York. Frosted throughout entire act.*

AT RISE.—*Discovered the four* MARCH *girls:* JO, *lying on the hearth rug, boyish attitude; her hands behind her head.* MEG, *sewing, sitting* R. *of* C. *table on the side toward the fire;* AMY, *also at the table, but more in the foreground, beside her sketching things, drawing-board on her lap, such as artists use, evidently copying the figure on the mantel-shelf, towards which she looks every few moments, making occasional erasures, showing desire to get copy as near the original as possible.* BETH, *cuddled down on a low stool near the chimney corner, knitting on a long blue army stocking and rocking small home-made doll cradle. Evident from the vacant easy-seat in front of the fire and the pair of slippers on the hearth-rug that some one is expected.*

NOTE.—*Tempo of first act must be quick.* JO *must set the pace.*

Medium Slow Curtain.

MUSIC.—*"Auld Lang Syne."* PP.

JO. *(Rolls over on stomach with elbows on stage,*

chin in hands) Christmas won't be Christmas without any presents.

MEG. *(Sewing carpet rags. Looking down at her dress, which is faded and shabby)* It's so dreadful to be poor!

AMY. *(Drawing, looking injured)* I don't think it's fair for some girls to have plenty of pretty things and others nothing at all.

BETH. *(Knitting, contentedly)* We've got Father and Mother and each other.

JO. *(Sadly)* We haven't got Father and shan't have him for a long time. I think it was splendid of him to go off to the war as a chaplain when he was too old to be drafted and not strong enough for a soldier. Wish I could go as a drummer, or a nurse, or a viva—viva—— *(Laughs)* What's its name?

MEG. You know why Mother proposed not having any presents this Christmas was because it's going to be a hard winter for everyone; and she thinks we ought not to spend money for pleasure, when our men are suffering so in the army.

JO. Well, the little we should spend wouldn't do any good. We've each got a *dollar*. *(Girls sigh)* I agree not to expect anything from you or Marmee, but I do want to buy Undine and Sintram for myself. I've wanted it so long.

BETH. *(Wistfully)* I planned to spend mine on new music.

AMY. *(Decidedly, examining pencil)* I shall get a nice box of drawing pencils. I really need them.

JO. *(Sits up)* Mother didn't say anything about *our* money, and she won't wish us to give up everything. Let's each buy what we want and have a little fun. I'm sure we work hard enough to earn it. *(Examines the heels of her shoes)*

MEG. I know I do, teaching those tiresome chil-

dren all day, when I'm longing to enjoy myself at
home.

Jo. You don't have half as hard a time as I do
with Aunt March. How would you like to be shut
up for hours with a nervous, fussy old lady, who
keeps calling "Josephine—Josephine!" *(Imitating*
AUNT MARCH. *Girls laugh)*—is never satisfied, and
worries you till you're ready to fly out of the window or cry?

BETH. I know it's naughty to fret, but I *do* think
that washing dishes and keeping things tidy is the
worst work in the world.

AMY. I don't believe any of you have as "tryinger"
(girls laugh) a time as I do, for you don't have to
go to school with impertinent girls, who laugh at your
dresses, insult you when your nose isn't nice, and
label your father if he isn't rich.

Jo. *(Laughing)* If you mean *libel*, I'd say so
and not talk as if papa was a pickle bottle.

AMY. *(With injured dignity)* I know what I
mean, and you needn't be "statirical" *(Laugh)* about
it. It's proper to use good words and to improve
your "vo-co-labilary." *(Laugh)*

Jo. *(Chuckling over* AMY's *two blunders and
bent on teasing her)* Girls, do you remember the
night Amy went to bed, with a clothes-pin on her
nose to uplift that offending feature?

AMY. *(As the others laugh, evidently nettled at
being teased)* Well, it wouldn't have been crooked
if you hadn't dropped me into the coal hod when I
was a baby. *(Slams down drawing board)* I intend
to take time by the fetlock and improve myself. *(All
laugh. Rise)* And you may laugh all you please, so
there!

Jo. Oh, indeed! *(Mockingly.)*

AMY. My one comfort is that Mother doesn't
take tucks in my dresses when I'm naughty.

MEG. Tucks in your dresses? Amy, what do you mean?

AMY. Maria Park's mother does, and, my dear, it's really dreadful, for sometimes she is *so bad* her frock is up to her *knees——* *(Pointing to knees)* and she can't come to school at all. *(Shout from all)*

Jo. Well, I call that mean.

AMY. So do I, and when I think of that *"degraderration,"* I feel that I can bear even my crooked nose and my purple gown with yellow skyrockets on it.

Jo. *(Disdainfully)* You do fuss so over clothes, Amy. I call it silly.

AMY. *(Takes up board, indignantly)* I don't intend to let myself be a *frump,* like *some* girls I know. *(Meaningly towards* Jo.*)*

Jo. Oh, dear me, let's be elegant, or die! *(Flops down again on back—head to audience. Begins to whistle "Yankee Doodle" softly and drums on the floor.)*

AMY. *(With reproving look toward* Jo*)* Jo does use such slang words. *(*Jo *whistles louder)* Don't, Jo, it's so boyish.

Jo. That's why I do it. *(Sits up.)* Thank Heaven, I've a boy's spirit under my bib and tucker.

(Ready Clock R.

AMY. I detest rude, unladylike girls.

Jo. I hate affected, niminy-piminy chits. *(*AMY *slams down board.)*

BETH. *(Sings)* "Birds in their little nests agree." *(*ALL *laugh and grow cheerful again.)*

MEG. *(Very dignified)* You are old enough to leave off boyish tricks, *Josephine.* It didn't matter so much when you were a little girl, but now you are so tall and turn up your hair, you should remember that you are a young lady.

Jo. *(Yanks off her hair net. Pulling down her*

hair, which hangs down her back in long, chestnut mane) I'm not, and if turning up my hair makes me one, I'll wear it in two tails till I'm twenty. I hate to think I've got to grow up, and be *Miss March,* and wear long gowns and be as prim as a *china-aster.* *(Sits up very straight and prim.)*

(Ready Door Bell.)

MEG. You needn't be prim—only girlish and——

JO. *(Breaking in)* Girlish! Humph! It's bad enough being a girl anyway, when I like boys' games and work and manners. *(Crossing one leg.)* I can't get over my disappointment in not being a boy, and it's worse than ever now, for I'm dying to go to the war and fight, with papa, and I can only stay at home and *knit* like a pokey old woman. *(Imitating* AUNT MARCH *again. Leans forward for* BETH'S *business.)*

BETH. *(Smoothing* JO'S *head with tender hand)* Poor Jo, it's too bad, but it can't be helped. So you must try to be content with making your name boyish and playing brother to us girls.

MEG. As for you, Amy—— *(*AMY *smiles, expecting praise—it changes to a martyr's expression and then a pout.)*—you are altogether too particular and prim. Your airs are funny now, but if you don't take care, you'll grow up an affected little goose. I like your nice manners and refined way of speaking, when you don't try to be elegant; but your absurd words are just as bad as Jo's slang.

(Clock strikes Five R.*)*

*(*MEG *puts work in bag.* AMY *goes to the window* C. *in a huff at being censured.* MEG *rises from chair seat.* JO, *during this general movement. on her knees with back to audience, rolls up hair—puts on net—makes long reach for apple without getting up—takes manuscript from chair—flops around into sitting position—back*

against chair and feet straight out. BETH *goes*
R.C.*)*

BETH. If Jo is a tomboy and Amy a goose, what
am I, please?
MEG. (R.C. *warmly*) You're a little dear, and
nothing else.

(MEG *takes ragbag to closet under stairway.* BETH
joins AMY *at baywindow* C. *As* MEG *reaches
foot of stairs, doorbell* R. *rings and* MEG *turns in
from staircase and crosses to hall door. It's
an old-fashioned bell on a spring and rings in
the kitchen off* R. HANNAH *enters* R. 3, *wiping
hand on apron, gets to center—pauses—looks,
and turns and stalks back.)*

MEG. I'll go, Hannah.

(HANNAH *exits* R. 3. MEG *exits to hall* L 1.)

VOICE. *(Outside)* Good evening, Miss Meg.
Here's a note for you.
MEG. Oh, thank you! *(Closes door and goes to
desk* L. *Shivers.)*
AMY. *(Half-tearfully to* BETH, *who has followed her to window and puts her arm around her)*
Jo does pick at me so. She laughs at my statues
and makes fun of my manners.
BETH. Dear old Jo, she can't understand your
liking to draw, because all she wants to do is to read
and write plays and stories.
AMY. *(Still injured)* Well, she needn't think I
like her old stories, 'cause I don't. *(She snaps this
at* Jo, *who pays no attention.* MEG *has opened letter,
letter in hand, vivacious and smiling.)*
MEG. *(Calls excitedly)* Jo, Jo, where are you?
(At desk.)

Jo. *(Mouth full of apple and evidently absorbed in her story)* Here.

MEG. *(Goes to fire-place and sits* L., *of* Jo *on the rug in front of armchair by fire-place)* Such fun— only see! A regular note of invitation from Mrs. Gardner. *(Waving the note and proceeding to read it.* BETH *comes down and listens, to back armchair at fire-place.* AMY *drops down slowly* C.*)* "Mrs. Gardner would be happy to see Miss March and Miss Josephine at a little dance on Christmas Eve." I'm sure Marmee will let us go. Now what shall we wear?

Jo. *(Mouth full of apple, of which she has taken a fresh bite)* What's the use of asking that, when you know we shall wear our poplins, because we haven't got anything else?

MEG. *(Sighing)* If I only had a silk!

Jo. I'm sure our pops look like silks and they are nice enough for us. Yours is as good as new. *(Turns to* MEG.*)* Oh, I forgot the burn in mine. Whatever shall I do? *(*AMY *has dropped down* C. *Right of table* C., *listening.)*

MEG. The burn?

Jo. Yes, I scorched it, standing with my back to the fire. *(*AMY *and* BETH *exclaim.)*

AMY. *(Turns, moves to front of table.)* Another of your boyish tricks. Jo, you are certainly "in-corr-rig-able." *(Gathers up pencils, etc., from table. Moving in front to* L. *of table* C.*)*

Jo. *(Too exercised about her frock to laugh at* AMY'S *blunder.)* That burn shows dreadfully.

BETH. *(Leaning over back of chair. Anxiously)* Can't you drop a little black velvet bow on it?

AMY. *(Over her shoulder.)* Wouldn't that look nice? A bow in the middle of her back! *(Goes up to* L. *of bay window* R.C. *to her table. Sits.)*

MEG. You'll just have to stay still and keep your

back out of sight. Your front is all right. How about your gloves?

Jo. *(Indifferently)* They're spoilt with lemonade, so I shall have to go without.

MEG. *(Horrified)* Oh, you must have gloves, or I won't go. You can't dance without them, and if you do, I should be so mortified!

Jo. Then I'll stay still. I don't care much for company dancing, anyhow. I like to fly round and cut capers.

MEG. Can't you *make* them do?

Jo. No! I'll tell you how we can manage—each wear *one good* one and *carry* a bad one.

MEG. *(Reluctantly)* Your hands are bigger than mine, and you will stretch my gloves dreadfully.

Jo. *(Taking up her Mss.)* Then I'll go without. I don't care what people say.

MEG. You may have it, you may. Only don't stain it, and do behave nicely. Don't put your hands behind you or say Christopher Columbus, or call things *"Plummy,"* will you?

Jo. *(Grinning.)* Don't worry about me, I'll be as prim as I can be.

MEG. Have you a nice pocket handkerchief?

Jo. Oh, yes, a plummy one.

MEG. *(Reproachfully)* Oh, Jo!

Jo. I mean, it's spandy nice. You're like Marmee. I believe she would ask if we had handkerchiefs if we were all running away from an earthquake.

(BETH *grins, goes up and joins* AMY C. *in window.* AMY *rises.*)

MEG. *(Rises, gets to* R.C.*)* It's one of her aristocratic tastes and quite proper. Mind you keep your back out of sight, Jo.

Jo. I know I shall forget. If you see me doing

anything wrong, just remind me by a wink, will you?
MEG. No, winking isn't ladylike.
Jo How *do* you learn to be so proper? (MEG
*goes to front of table, stops, looks at her reproach-
fully,* Jo *opening her manuscript again and settling
down to write.)* All right, all right. Now go and
answer your note and let me finish The Witch's
Curse.

(MEG *goes to desk* L. BETH *and* AMY *wave and
call "oo-hoo" to* LAURIE *from window* C. MEG
waves from desk—window L.)

BETH. *(R. of* AMY *at* C. *window)* There goes
Laurie on his new horse. *(All except* Jo *wave hands
to* LAURIE *and call "Laurie.")* How well that boy
rides!
AMY. *(Turning to girls.)* Laurie is a perfect
Cyclops, isn't he?

(BETH *goes to piano, smiling.)*

Jo. *(Looking up from her work, indignantly)*
How *can* you say that, when he's got *both* his
eyes——
AMY. *(Coming down* C. *a little)* I didn't say
anything about his *eyes,* and I don't see why you
need fire up when I admire his riding.
Jo. *(Roaring)* Oh, my goodness! That little
goose means a *centaur,* and she calls him a *Cyclops!*
AMY. You needn't be so rude. It's only a "lapse
of lingy," as our teacher says.

(BETH *then starts in to sing to stop the little wrangle
—"The Land of the Leal"—one verse—*AMY
and MEG *join in softly.* BETH *plays a few
chords after; then exits to dining room* R. *This
is Father's favorite song, and it saddens them all*

*for a moment. Jo flops on to her stomach on the
floor at fireplace and writes manuscript furi-
ously. AMY, at her table in the bay window,
occupies herself with a clay figure she is modeling. MEG goes to R. of table C. and takes up
work basket. BETH gets bread, toasting fork
and plate and comes directly back; sits on rug
before fire.)*

Jo. *(Rising)* Well, I've finished "The Witch's
Curse," Meg. We've got to rehearse our parts in
costume and with the scenery and get used to 'em.
(Goes to R.C.) There's lots to do about that play
before Christmas night. *(Jo marches up and down
the room, R.C., her hands behind her back.)*

MEG. *(Who has resumed her embroidery.)* I
don't mean to act any more after this time.

Jo. *(Stops R.C.)* What?

MEG. I'm getting too old for such things.

Jo. *(Down stage R.)* You won't stop, I know, as
long as you can trail around in a long gown, with
your hair down, and wear gold paper jewelry. Why,
you're the best actress we've got, and there'll be an
end to everything if you quit the boards. *(Turns
R.)* Well, come here, Amy, and do the fainting
scene, for you're as stiff as a poker in that.

AMY. I can't help it. *(Rises. Comes down R.C.
by MEG's chair.)* I never saw anyone faint, and I
don't choose to make myself all black and blue,
tumbling flat as you do. If I can go down easily,
I'll drop, if I can't, I shall fall into a chair and be
graceful. *(Funny awkward pose.)*

Jo. Oh! Oh, do it this way—— *(Throws manuscript down.)* clasp your hands so, and stagger
across the room, crying frantically, "Roderigo, save
me, save me! Save me!" *(Jo goes to L., throws
herself against door L.1. Climax last "Save me."
AMY works down stage to R.C. Jo does this, with*

*melodramatic scream and with much intensity, turns
—nonchalantly with back to door as she says)*
There you are—now you do it.

*(Amy follows, poking out her hands stiffly and go-
ing to L.C. bus.—jerking herself along as if she
went by machinery.)*

Amy. *(Perfectly expressionless in face and
voice.)* "Roderigo, save me! Save me! Save me!"
Jo. *(In despair.)* Scream, Amy, scream as if
you were calling for help.
Amy. "Ow!" *(Her scream is an "Ow" of dis-
tress, far more than of melodramatic anguish.)*

*(Jo business of disgust. Meg roars; Jo groans and
makes despairing gesture. Beth, toasting bread
before the fire, lets it burn while she watches the
fun.)*

Jo. *(Throws up hands as she strides up stage.)*
It's no use—no use. Do the best you can when the
time comes, and if the audience laughs, don't blame
me. *(Amy goes up and sits on lower step of stairs
in a huff—chin in hands, elbows on knees.)* Come
on, Meg. Do the incantation scene with the love
potion!
Meg. *(Rummaging in her work basket, produces
a small bottle, rising, she holds the bottle well for·
ward, to attract attention, and half chants:)*

> "Hither I come
> From my airy home
> Afar in the silver moon.
>   *(Holds out bottle.)*
> Take the magic spell
> And use it well
> Or its power will vanish soon."

Jo. *(As* Ernest *the lover, goes to* Meg, *snatches the wooden dagger from table, and kneeling before* Meg, *declaims)* "By me trusty *sword. (Dagger up.)* I swear that Ernest L'Estrange— shall pay, pay royally, for this priceless gift, *(Dagger back.)* a love potion with which to win the lovely Zara." *(Takes vial with deep bow. Bus. of looking at each other to see whose cue it is. With a total change of voice.)* Come on, come on, Amy, that's your cue.

Amy. Oh, dear, I never can remember. *(Rises quickly and comes* D.L. Amy *recites in a perfectly expressionless voice.)* " 'Tis like a dream, so strange, so terrible. *(Looks between* Meg *and* Jo. Jo *groans and handles the dagger meaningly.)* He whom I thought so gentle and so true is stained with fearful crimes,—poor murdered lady—have I escaped a fate like thine? *(Jo rises, stamps foot and goes* R.C.*)* Ah, I hear his step. Now, heart, be firm." *(Bus. of hand on heart—wrong side— corrects it.)*

Jo. *(Parenthetically)* I'm the villain now, remember. *(Goes to* Amy L.C. *a little up stage. Voice changes to melodramatic threatening.* Jo. *grasps* Amy's *arm, frightening her.)* "Proud lady, if thou wilt not love, I'll make thee learn to *fear* the heart thou hast so scornfully cast away. Thou shalt rue the day when Count Rudolpho asked and was refused. But I will win thee yet—and then—Beware!" *(Rolls "*R.*" Turns away, folds arms and drops head—tragic pose.)*

Amy. *(Jo snaps fingers under her folded arms and pantomimes "Go on." Amy gasps, so interested she forgets she's acting, suddenly recovers. Voice still expressionless, also a bit uncertain about her lines.)* "Do thy worst, murderer. Spirits will watch over me—*(Hand over head.)* and thou canst not harm. Adieu (Adoo) my lord"! Adieu.

(Bows low—backs away to L. AMY *uses perfectly sweet, pleasant voice in her acting.)*

JO. Don't say "adoo"—say "adyeux"—let the "eu" stop in your nose. *(AMY feels nose, sits* L. *on chair below desk* L.*)* The next scene is in Norma's cave.

MEG. *(Rises and goes quickly behind the wing-chair* R. *and crosses from it, bent over and with hands clasped and raised like an old witch. As* NORMA— *cracked voice.* JO *goes up stage* L. *and takes pose as villain and works up this scene with* MEG.*)* "Sinful man, thy hour of reckoning has come. 'Twas *I* who bore thy murdered wife to a quiet grave and raised her spirit to affright and haunt thee. I warned Hugo and betrayed thee to his power. Thy victims are avenged and Norma's work is done. Her curse has sealed thy doom. Farewell! Farewell! *(Backing up to back of armchair at fireplace. Ending with a cackling, sinister laugh)* Ha! Ha! Ha!" *(Disappears behind chair.)*

JO. *(As the villain,* RUDOLPHO, *up* L.C.*)* "Help, help, the ghosts! They torture me. The souls of the murdered, they haunt me! See! See! *(Stamps her foot and points suddenly* L., *and* AMY *jumps and swings her feet to* L.*)* The demons gather about. How fast they come, how fast! Old Norma is muttering her spells. Let me go! Let me go! *(Comes down stage* L.C. *in a desperate melodramatic struggle with herself.)* Hugo! Norma! Zara! Pity, pity! Let not Ernest L'Estrange reach me!—Ah!"

(As if stabbed—does funny flop—in a heap. MEG *comes down* R.C. JO *sits up, rubbing her elbows, enjoying the sensation she has caused.* GIRLS *much impressed, not sure* JO *hasn't killed her-self.)*

MEG. *(Coming down to R. of table C.)* It's the best we've had yet. *(Sits R. of table C.)*

BETH. *(In awe.)* I don't see how you can act and write such splendid things, Jo. You're a regular Shakespeare. *(BETH has taken bread from toasting fork and unconsciously slips fork into a slipper which she holds out toward the fire.)*

JO. *(Modestly, gets to L. of table.)* Not quite! *(Rubbing her elbow.)* But I think it would be great for Meg and me to go on the stage. We could make lots of money, *perhaps,* and it's a very gay life. I shall write tragic plays and be a second Siddons. I'd love to do Macbeth, if we only had a trap door for Banquo. I've always wanted to do the killing part. *(Makes sudden turn R. and stamp of foot which makes MEG, who is sitting R. of table, jump. Mutters—in stage whisper:)* "Is this a dagger that I see before me?"

(MEG shrinks with fear at the reality of Jo's acting—funny turn in chair. Jo imitates traditional bus. going front of table. MEG catches sight of slipper.)

MEG. *(Acting first part of line.)* No, it's the toasting fork. *(Laughing.)* With mother's old shoe on it. Beth's stage-struck.

(General scream of laughter from all. Sound of the street door. Enter MRS. MARCH 1st. Comes to L.C.)

MRS. MARCH. Glad to find you so merry, my girls. *(At door L.)*

ALL. Marmee!

(MRS. MARCH goes to C., surrounded by girls. AMY L. of MARMEE, takes handbag and goes L. and

puts it in closet. MEG, at her R., takes shawl and bonnet and goes R. and back of table C. to closet L.U. After greeting C. JO goes to fireplace and pokes fire, BETH puts toast down and takes off MARMEE'S arctics—which MEG comes, gets and takes into dining room and flies back to MARMEE, who has kept on crossing to fireplace where she sits in armchair.)

MRS. MARCH. Well, dearies, how have you got on to-day?

JO. *(On BETH'S little seat below fireplace.)* Oh, we've had a "plummy" day.

MRS. MARCH. There was so much to do. getting the boxes for the soldiers ready, that I didn't come home to dinner.

BETH. We missed you, Marmee.

MRS. MARCH. *(In chair at fireplace.)* Has anyone called, Beth? How is your cold, Meg?

MEG. It's better, Marmee.

MRS. MARCH. Jo, you look tired to death. Come and kiss me, baby. *(Sits in armchair. BETH places slippers. AMY at arm of chair R. kisses her. MEG takes slippers, kneeling L. of MRS. MARCH. BETH and MEG put on mother's slippers, putting her shoes by the fire—and a small foot-stool under her feet. AMY at back of chair R. of mother, putting things to rights. General bustle of welcome for the queen of the household.)* Girls, I heard from Father to-day.

(Position: JO on BETH'S stool at lower side of fireplace. AMY standing at R. of armchair back. BETH in front of armchair to the R. on the floor. MEG at L. of armchair to the L. on the floor.)

JO. *(Rapturously)* A letter! A letter! Three cheers for Father.

MRS. MARCH.   No, not a letter, dear, but a message from one of our soldiers who has been sent home on sick leave.   Father is well and thinks he shall get through the cold season better than he feared.   He sends all sorts of loving messages to his Little Women.

AMY.   It must be very disagreeable to sleep in a tent, and eat all sorts of bad-tasting things, and drink out of a *canteen*.

(Quiet snicker from Jo at AMY's blunder, and even MRS. MARCH hides a smile.   BETH comes quickly to the rescue, by breaking in.)

BETH.   When will he come home, Marmee?

MRS. MARCH.   Not for many months, dear, unless he is sick.   He will stay and do his work faithfully, as long as he can, and we won't ask for him back a moment sooner than he can be spared.

(Enter HANNAH R. 3—dining room.)

HANNAH.   *(L. of armchair at fireplace)*   Miss' March, will you have your tea now?

MRS. MARCH.   If you please, Hannah.   *(Ring at door.   MEG rises and starts.)*

(Bell R.   NOTE: Old-fashioned doorbell rings in dining room R.3 when pulled L.1st.)

HANNAH.   *(Going to hall door L.1.)*   I'll go, mum.

(Exits to hall.)

BROOKE.   *(Outside.)*   Well, Hannah!

HANNAH.   *(Outside.)*   Oh, Mr. Brooke.   *(Returning, announcing)*   Mister Brooke, mum.

(MRS. MARCH rises and goes to R.C.   Jo rises quickly and joins MEG.   Enter MR. BROOKE, holds hat

HANNAH *goes from room and exits to dining room. Position:* MRS. MARCH C. JOHN L.C. MEG, JO, BETH *and* AMY *in line up* R.C. AMY *extreme* R.)

MRS. MARCH. *(Holding out her hand.)* Good afternoon, Mr. Brooke.

(As they line up, MEG *primps a little.* JO *glares at her.)*

BROOKE. Good afternoon, Mrs. March. Good afternoon—*(To* GIRLS. BROOKE *shakes hands with* MRS. MARCH C. MEG *greets* BROOKE *with shy manner.* JO *greets* BROOKE *with boyish nod.* AMY *greets* BROOKE *with affected little bow.* BETH *greets* BROOKE *with little, old-fashioned curtsey.* BROOKE *is particularly impressive in his manner to* MEG, *who acts a little conscious.* JO *a bit stand-offish, the little girls shy and interested.)* I come as an emissary both of peace and of war. Laurie begs permission to attend the dress rehearsal, and I have come for those hospital supplies. They must go out tonight.

MRS. MARCH. Certainly, I'll get them directly. Girls, why not let Mr. Brooke and the Laurences come to your rehearsal?

MEG. *(Comes forward a little.)* Mercy, no, Mother, men are positively excluded. Laurie sneaked in our Pickwick Club, but even he can't wheedle me into allowing men at our rehearsai.

JO. Well, I'm sure Teddy won his Pickwick honors, sitting on a ragbag in a stuffy closet for an hour, while you and Amy wrangled about admitting him.

AMY. *(As* BROOKE *listens, visibly amused.)* We don't want men at our little performances. They're sure to laugh—and I never can bear to be laughed at.

BROOKE. *(Trying to keep his face sober.)* Not a laugh, I swear it. Miss Meg, won't you relent?

MEG. No, indeed, if men are admitted, I sha'n't play.

JO. What do you say, Beth? Remember, it's our Laurie.

BETH. *(With most unwonted enthusiasm.)* I say he shall come, and his grandpa, too, if he likes.

JO. *(Slapping leg.)* Bully for you, Beth!

MRS. MARCH *and* MEG. Jo! *(*MEG *gives* JO *reproving look.)*

JO. *(Turn to* MEG.*)* Meg, be a good sort and give in.

(READY BELL.

MEG. *(Wavering)* I'll think about it.

JO. *(Goes to back, upsets chair at back of table c.)* Well, hurry up. I must set the stage and get into my costume.

(Exit Jo *upstairs with a rush.)*

MRS. MARCH. *(Goes to library door* R.I.*)* Beth, Amy, help me collect the hospital things, please, and Meg, entertain Mr. Brooke while we are gone.

(Exit MRS. MARCH, BETH *and* AMY *into Study.* MEG *gives a little start after mother and sisters as if to say: "Don't leave me alone with* MR. BROOKE." *Then turns and gives an embarrassed little laugh as her eyes meet* BROOKE'S. BROOKE *up stage* L. *replaces chair back of table, comes down to* MEG, R.C., *and takes folded manuscript paper from pocket and hands it to* MEG.*)*

BROOKE. Here's the translation of the little French song Laurie promised you, Miss March.

MEG. *(Looking it over.)* How very sweet, but

this isn't Laurie's writing. Did you make the translation for me, Mr. Brooke?

BROOKE. The song has always been a favorite of mine—and——

(His sentence is interrupted by the furious ringing of the doorbell and rat tat tat on the brass knocker.)

(BELL R. *VERY LOUD.*

LAURIE. *(Outside.)* What ho—within there—What ho!

BROOKE. My soul!

MEG. Gracious me, what is that?

(Enter HANNAH, *rushing through room to answer door.)*

HANNAH. The saints preserve us! Is the house on fire?

(Exits to hall. AMY *and* BETH *enter from study.* MRS. MARCH *following more leisurely, her arms filled with the supplies.)*

AMY, BETH *and* MRS. MARCH. *(Speaking together.)* What's the matter, Hannah? What is it?

LAURIE. *(In hall.)* Hello, Hannah!

HANNAH. Oh, it's Mr. Laurie.

(Enter LAURIE, *flushed and breathless, his arms filled with flowers, an unframed picture under his arm, cap in hand.)*

LAURIE. Good afternoon, everybody! *(*HANNAH *re-enters room and goes to dining room, where she exits. Beaming on the boy.* MRS. MARCH *goes to* R. *of table. Laughing. Puts bundle on table.*

LAURIE *presenting flowers to* MRS. MARCH.*)* For you, Madam Mother, with grandpa's compliments.

MRS. MARCH. Oh, thank you, Laurie. *(Sits L. of C. table.)*

LAURIE. *(Throws cap in chair L.)* Well, I've come for the rehearsal. How about it?

MEG. *(R.C.)* We'll see.

*(BETH takes vase from mantel, goes into din-
   ing room, returning quickly to back of table C.
   AMY joins her mother—L. of table C.)*

JO. *(Calling from above.)* Hurry up, Meg, time for you and Amy.

MEG. Yes, Jo, I'm coming. *(Smiles shyly at BROOKE, who is R.)*

*(Goes back and upstairs. MRS. MARCH has put the
   flowers in the vase. Now rises and crosses to
   fireplace. BROOKE takes them from her and
   places on mantel. BETH goes up C.)*

LAURIE. *(L.C. Handing AMY the picture.)* Here's the Madonna you wanted to copy, little Raphael.

AMY. *(L.C. Sincerely, goes to him, taking it eagerly.)* Thank you so much, Laurie. I've tried to draw it from memory, but the woman's face is not good. It's too beautiful for me to draw; but the baby was better, and I love it so much. I love to think He was a little child once, for then I don't seem so far away, and that helps me.

*(This speech should be spoken so directly to LAURIE
   that the others do not hear. LAURIE'S reply in
   the same way.)*

LAURIE. *(Gently, her mood evidently chiming in*

with certain longings of his own.) Try again, dear.
Even Raphael didn't succeed with his first Madonna.
  Jo. *(Calling from above)* Come on up, Amy,
time for you.

(CRASH READY LEFT UPSTAIRS.)

  AMY. *(Starts to run, then walks up very ladylike.)* All right.

(AMY exits with picture upstairs.)

  LAURIE. *(Calling from the foot of stairs.)* Jo,
Jo, come down quick. I've something to tell you.
  JO. *(Still from above.)* Go away, Teddy, I'm
busy !
  BETH. *(Joining* LAURIE, *and both going to bay
window. To* LAURIE) Jo's busy setting the stage,
Laurie. See the Christmas roses? *(Turning to the
window.)* How beautiful they are! You didn't
think they would bloom.

*(*BETH *picks a rosebud and fastens it in his but-
tonhole.)*

  BROOKE. *(*R.C. *To* MRS MARCH, *who goes to
front of* c. *table. Glancing upstairs.)* Doesn't look
very hopeful about the rehearsal, Mrs. March.
  MRS. MARCH. *(Smiling.)* I wish you might see
the fun, but Meg is getting a little conscious over
their stage frolics and I'm afraid Jo can't tease her
into admitting you.

*(*BROOKE *goes* R. *A long, wailing scream from* AMY.
  *Crash upstairs—*AMY *and* Jo's *voices.* AMY
  cries. Jo *scolds.* MEG *laughs.)*

  LAURIE. Jupiter Ammon! *(As* MRS. MARCH

starts toward stairs, old HANNAH, *evidently frightened at the noise, appears in the doorway* R. 3. *She
is floury and her hands are rolled in her apron.)*
All serene here, Hannah. Racket was upstairs.
     HANNAH. It's them girls, rehearsing again, and
the Missus never says a word.

*(*HANNAH *throws up hands, exits grumbling.* BETH
     comes to C. *back of table.* LAURIE *goes down*
     R.C. *to* BROOKE. MRS. MARCH L. MEG *has
     started to come down. She is laughing and
     carries her witch's cloak and beard as she runs
     down.)*

     MRS. MARCH. *(*L.*)* Anyone hurt, Meg?
     MEG. *(Coming downstairs and to* L.*)* Oh, no.
The pasteboard tower fell just as Ernest was trying to carry off Zara. They all came down together. *(*ALL *roar.)*
     LAURIE. Was Jo furious?
     MEG. *(Down* L.*)* I didn't wait to find out. All
I could see was Amy's head and Jo's russet boots.

MRS. MARCH L. *with* MEG. MEG *puts cloak, hat,
     beard on chair at desk* L. JO *stamps down the
     stairs, scolding under breath at* AMY'S *stupid-
     ity—Roderigo costume. Black satin breeches
     and jerkin; flowing cape, chapeau and russet-
     top boots, which keep falling down, at sight of
     which* BROOKE *and* LAURIE *roar.* MEG *goes* L.
     near desk.)

     JO. *(*L.C. *Pulling cloak around her.)* Be quiet,
you bad boy. I thought you had gone home.
     LAURIE. *(*C.*)* Where on earth did you get the
boots?
     JO. *(*C. *Putting bootleg up and holding out one
leg for them to see. Looking down at them*

proudly.) Aren't they great? I got 'em from a friend who knows a lady who knows an *actor.*

BROOKE. They're certainly fetching.

MEG. *(L. Annoyed at Jo's appearance.)* Oh, go and dress, Jo. *(Jo makes funny turn and hat falls off)* You're ridiculous in that costume.

Jo. All right, don't bother, I will. Wait, Teddy, I'll be back in a jiffy.

LAURIE. All right, Jo.

(Back of table C. Exit Jo, falling upstairs over her boots and stepping into her cloak—on second part of stairs.)

BROOKE. Then there will be no rehearsal?

MEG. Not before to-morrow. It will take time to repair the ravages to Zara's tower.

BROOKE. *(Taking package of supplies from table C. under his arm, coming C.)* I must hurry along. I'll stop at your grandfather's on my way back, Laurie, and leave that Latin book for you.

LAURIE. All right, *Professor. (At foot of stairs.)*

BROOKE. Good-by, Mrs. March.

(BROOKE shakes hands with MRS. MARCH L.C. Starts to shake hands with MEG, who is L. She moves to L. of table C, hesitates, as he sees MEG's shy embarrassment, then goes L., gets his hat from chair below desk, opens door L.I. and turns and says good-by to MEG, in confidential understanding manner. Exits; LAURIE gets this business and smiles. MEG goes up to L. window to look out after BROOKE. After BROOKE's exit, MRS. MARCH sits L. of table C.)

(VOICE READY L

LAURIE. Won't some of you come for a drive? Brooke has been making me study hard all day. Beth, run up and ask Jo and Amy to get ready, and you come along, too.

BETH. Thank you, Laurie, we'd love to go. I'll tell Jo and Amy.

(Exit BETH upstairs.)

LAURIE. How about you, Meg?

MEG. Much obliged, but I'm busy. *(Goes to R. of table C. and takes up sewing.)*

LAURIE. *(Leaning affectionately over the back of MRS. MARCH's chair L. of table C.)* Anything I can do for you, Madam Mother?

(BELL R.)

MRS. MARCH. *(Bell rings—HANNAH goes to hall.)* No, thank you. *(Pause.)* Except call at the office, if you'll be passing, dear. It's our day for a letter, and Father is as regular as the sun.

(VOICE L.I.E. & TELEGRAM.)

VOICE. *(Outside L.I.)* Telegram for Mrs. March. Sign here.

(HANNAH re-enters with telegram, which she hands to MRS. MARCH, as if she feared it would explode.)

HANNAH. *(L.)* It's one of them horrid telegraph things, ma'am. *(MRS. MARCH rises, frightened—hesitates—then smiles and takes it, opens and reads it, L.C.—almost faints)*

MRS. MARCH. Girls! Girls! Your Father——

(LAURIE places chair for her. MEG goes to mother, places her in chair L. of table C.—MEG R. of her

—paper falling to the floor. HANNAH *supports
her.* LAURIE *rushes to dining room for water.)*

MEG. *(Dropping on knees beside her.)* Marmee,
what is it? *(*MEG *calls out)* Girls, girls, come
quick!

*(*LAURIE *returns to back of table with the water,
which* MEG *gives to her mother. Three girls
come rushing down the stairs.* Jo *last. She is
in her dress.)*

BETH. Marmee!
AMY. Marmee!
MEG. It's that telegram.

*(*JO *picks up telegram and reads it in frightened
voice.)*

JO. *(*L.C.*)* "Your husband is very ill."
ALL. Marmee!
JO. "Come at once. S. Hale. Blank Hospital.
Washington." *(Goes to her mother* L.*)*

*(*LAURIE *withdraws to bay window.)*

MRS. MARCH. *(Stretching out her arms to her
girls.)* I must go, I must go at once! It may be too
late——
ALL. Marmee. *(*GIRLS *sob.)*
MRS. MARCH. Oh, children, children, help me to
bear it!

*(*GIRLS *cluster around her sobbing, "Marmee,
Father."* HANNAH *at right, back of table,* Jo L.
and AMY *at* R. *of chair.* MEG *kneeling on floor
to* R. *of* MARMEE. BETH *kneeling on floor to
L. of* MARMEE.*)*

HANNAH. *(Half sobbing.)* The Lord help the

dear man. I won't waste no time a cryin', but get
your things ready right away, mum!

(Exit HANNAH upstairs.)

MRS. MARCH. *(Pulling herself together.)* She
is right; there's no time for tears now.

ALL. Marmee!

MRS. MARCH. Be calm, girls, and let Mother
think. *(BETH and AMY drop upstage to foot of
stairs. JO L., MEG in front of table C.)* Jo, give me
a pencil and paper. Where's Laurie?

*(JO gets a pencil and paper from desk L. MEG turns
R. for LAURIE.)*

LAURIE. *(Down R. of table to C., coming to her
quickly from window where he has been standing
with his back turned.)* Here, ma'am, oh, let me do
something!

MRS. MARCH. Send a telegram saying I'll come
at once. The next train leaves at six o'clock, I think.
I'll take that one. *(She scribbles a note hastily, Jo
looking over her shoulder.)*

LAURIE. What else? The horses are ready, I can
go anywhere, do anything.

MRS. MARCH. *(Handing him the note she has
just folded.)* Leave this note at Aunt March's.
Now go, dear *(LAURIE goes L.)*, and don't kill yourself driving at a desperate pace.

(Exit LAURIE, front door L.I.)

JO. *(L.C.)* Mother, you ask that old dragon for
money?

MRS. MARCH. Jo, I had to. I haven't five dollars in my purse.

Jo. Her rheumatism's been bad to-day, and she's sure to refuse. *(Goes to L.)*

Mrs. March. *(Quietly)* Father needs me, and some way will be provided. *(Starts to make memorandum.)* I cannot think that Aunt March will refuse at a time like this.

Jo. Well, you've got more faith in her than I have. She always croaks if you ask her for a ninepence. *(Stops and ponders, at desk L., puts hands on her head, shuts her lips firmly at last, as if decided upon her course, obviously fishing for an excuse. Coming down.)* Hadn't I better go over to the hospital rooms, Marmee, and tell them you'll not be there to-morrow?

Mrs. March. *(Writing on slip of paper.)* Yes, dear. *(Jo goes to closet and gets cloak, bonnet and mittens.)* If you will, I had quite forgotten—and, Jo, on your way please stop at the drug store and get these things. *(Handing her the paper. Exit Jo hall door L.I.)* Amy, tell Hannah to get down the leather trunk. *(Exit Amy, upstairs.)* Beth, run over and ask Mr. Laurence for a couple of bottles of old wine; I'm not too proud to beg for Father. *(Grabbing shawl and hood from closet, exit Beth front door L.I. Mrs. March rises and starts up. Meg goes up R. of table to back.)* And Meg, come and help me find my things, for I'm half bewildered.

(As Mrs. March gets to foot of stairs, she staggers. Meg catches her with frightened cry of:)

Meg. Marmee! Now, Marmee, you come right over here and sit by the fire. *(Leads her over to armchair at fireplace.)* And let me find your things. You will need all the rest you can get. *(Gets her in chair.)* Hannah will help me pack and I'll bring you some tea.

(Exit MEG *to dining room.* HANNAH *and* AMY *come down the stairs, bumping the trunk.* HANNAH, *grumbling and protesting. is bearing the lower, heavier weight of the trunk.* AMY, *expostulating, is evidently giving little help in carrying, as she has hold of the handle in relaxed fashion.* HANNAH *jerks trunk as she reaches foot of stairs,* AMY *stumbles down last three steps.)*

HANNAH. *(Coming downstairs.)* This is a lot of nonsense!

AMY. Mother said to bring the trunk down here.

HANNAH. *(Still grumbling)* Sakes alive! Guess I packed trunks before you were born. Where will you have this, mum? *(Reaching* R.C. *Turning to* MRS. MARCH *and indicating trunk)* Here?

MRS. MARCH. Oh, no, in the dining room, please.

*(*HANNAH *jerks trunk, nearly taking* AMY *off her feet.)*

AMY. Hannah, you're always so *precipitious.*

(Exit HANNAH *and* AMY *dining room* R. 3. BETH *enters* L.I., *holding door open for* MR. LAURENCE, *who enters directly after her.* MR. LAURENCE *is loaded down, two bottles, cobwebby, of old wine, a muffler, the old-time woolen square, a man's shawl, such as Lincoln wore; a gay dressing gown and a pair of gay knitted slippers.)*

MR. LAURENCE. *(Gives* BETH *his hat.* BETH *puts it on chair* L., *takes off her shawl and hood and places same on seat under stairway, and goes at back to mother's* R. *as* MRS. MARCH *rises to meet him.* MR. LAURENCE *trying to shake hands, but finding it impossible, as in addition to his gifts he has his gold-*

headed walking stick under his arm.) My dear
madam *(Coming to c.),* I am deeply grieved at this
sad news; but we will hope for the best.

MRS. MARCH. It is all we can do, sir.

MR. LAURENCE. *(Handing her the wine.)* This
is the wine you did me the honor to ask for, madam.
*(Reaching back into his hip pocket, he produces a
small flask, which he holds up to the light, after the
manner of a connoisseur.)* Here is some old peach
brandy, which may prove useful! *(Hands her the
flask.)*

MRS. MARCH. Oh, thank you, Mr. Laurence.
You are so kind.

MR. LAURENCE. Don't mention it, I beg of you.
Hospital wards are often cold and cheerless, so I
have ventured to offer my dressing gown—*(Handing her the gown)*—and this heavy shawl. *(Handing her the shawl.)* This muffler—*(Gives her the
muffler)*—and these warm slippers—*(Handing her
the slippers, which he dangles in mid-air as she takes
them.)*—not beautiful, madam, but most comfortable, I assure you.

*(*MRS. MARCH *is tearful and yet almost laughing,
at the way he has loaded her down. She needs
her handkerchief, but her hands are full.* BETH
steps quietly over to her mother and dries MRS.
MARCH'S *eyes with her own handkerchief,* MR.
LAURENCE *turns L. a little.)*

MRS. MARCH. Mr. Laurence, you are so thought-
ful, so kind. I don't know how to thank you.

*(*MR. LAURENCE *is evidently much moved. He
reaches back to his coat-tail pocket, and produces a large white handkerchief, faultlessly
folded, which he proceeds to shake out; bus.
and blows his nose violently.)*

MR. LAURENCE. Don't try to, ma'am, don't try. *(Turns to her.)* It will be a long, hard journey for a woman alone. May I offer myself as an escort?

MRS. MARCH. Mr. Laurence, I couldn't think of letting you take that long journey. If you will only look after my girls when I am gone——

MR. LAURENCE. As if they were my own, ma'am. I promise you. *(Slight pause, and his next words are fraught with meaning. Puts his hand into his breast pocket.)* Is there anything else I can do? Are you supplied with all the necessities?

MRS. MARCH. *(Hesitating, as she gets his meaning that he will provide funds, if needed, evidently holding to her faith that Aunt March will come to the rescue.)* Yes, thank you. I am sure all my wants will be met.

MR. LAURENCE. Don't hesitate to call upon me in any emergency. *(He gets an idea, rubs his hands and goes to door L.I.)* I will be back directly. *(Takes hat, opens door, throws end of muffler over shoulder, exits L.I.)* Brrr——

(MRS. MARCH stands with her arms filled with his gifts, looks down at the slippers and smiles sadly.)

MRS. MARCH. *(Speaking softly to herself.)* Oh, the kind, generous gentleman! *(Turns to BETH and lays the things across her arms.)* Meg—ah—— *(So confused she calls "BETH, MEG")* Beth, take these to Meg, please, and tell her to pack them all carefully. *(Emphasize the last word to express her tender appreciation.)*

BETH. Yes, Marmee! I will.

(BETH exits, leaving door open into dining room. MRS. MARCH returns to her chair by the fire while this dialogue is heard off stage, takes off

*slippers—pulls on shoes, turns chair in toward
fireplace and closes her eyes and rests.)*

HANNAH. *(Off.)* Miss Beth, your Ma won't
need those things no more'n a cat. What would
she do with them in a hospital, child?
BETH. Mr. Laurence brought them for Father.

(READY SLEIGH BELLS, L.)

MEG. Please put them in the tray, Hannah, and
Beth, go find mother's big shawl. She'll need that
for traveling. Tell Amy to get together her bonnet,
gloves and things, while I take in her tea.
HANNAH. My bread is riz, but I'll be right back
and finish your ma's trunk, Miss Meg.

*(MEG enters from dining room, as MR. BROOKE en-
ters, in haste, hat in hand, from hall door. He
closes door and places hat on chair below, desk
L. MEG, holding a tea tray in both hands and
a pair of overshoes caught in one hand, meets
BROOKE just back of table C. At sight of BROOKE
she drops the rubbers and almost the tea, which
BROOKE rescues. BROOKE grabs opposite edge
of tea tray. MRS. MARCH, her back to the
room, sitting with her head resting on her hand,
is unconscious of either person.)*

BROOKE. *(Quietly)* I'm very sorry to hear of this,
Miss March. Mr. Laurence has commissions for
me in Washington, and I have come to offer myself
as escort to your mother.
MEG. *(Both holding tray.)* How kind you are.
It will be such a relief to feel that she has you to
take care of her. Thank you very, very much.
*(They stand looking at one another for a minute.
JOHN leans toward her. MEG is evidently confused.*

for her next words are spoken hurriedly) Oh, I'm afraid this tea is getting cold—won't you come and speak to Mother? *(Turning toward Mother.)*

BROOKE. *(Releasing her hand.)* No, I won't trouble your mother now, but will be back with the sleigh in time. *(Bus.:* BROOKE *gets hat, opens door* L.I., *looks and almost inaudibly says:)* Goodby. *(To* MEG*)*

(SLEIGH BELLS.)

*(*MEG *carries the tea to her mother.)*

MEG. Here's your tea, Marmee, dear.

MRS. MARCH. *(Taking cup.)* Thank you, Meg. Has Laurie returned from Aunt March yet?

MEG. Not yet, dear! *(*MEG *goes to window up* C., *hearing sleigh bells.)* That may be Laurie now. *(Looking out.)* No, it's Aunt March herself, Mother—— *(*MRS. MARCH *rises)* I'll let her in. *(Starts toward door as she speaks.)* Mr. Brooke was just here and will act as your escort to-night to Washington—— *(*MRS. MARCH *puts teacup on little stand* R.*)*

(SLEIGH BELLS STOP. VOICE HEARD.)

VOICE. "WHOA!" "Whoa!"

*(*MEG *hastens into hall to admit* AUNT MARCH.*)*

MEG. Oh, Aunt March.

AUNT MARCH. *(Ad lib outside.)* Oh, my knee, be careful, etc. *(Enter* AUNT MARCH, *comes* C., MEG L.C. *Very crabbed and short in manner, especially so after any show of tenderness.)* What's this, what's this I hear? March sick in Washington? Serves him right, serves him right. I always said it was absurd for him to go into the army.

and perhaps next time he'll take my advice. *(In front of table a little to L. of C. table.)*

MEG. Father did what he thought was right, Aunt March. *(Down stage L.)*

MRS. MARCH. *(Pushing forward an easy chair R. of table.)* Won't you sit down, Aunt March?

AUNT MARCH. *(Snappishly)* No, I won't sit down. *(Turns away.)* A stronger man could have done more. Shouldn't have gone, shouldn't have gone. I knew he'd get fever or something; never did know how to take care of himself, or his money. You needn't be begging me for help now if he had. He'd give his last dollar or the shirt off his back to the first man who asked him. Where would I be now if I'd done the same, I'd like to know?

(READY LIGHTS.

MRS. MARCH. I'm sorry to ask you for money, Aunt March, but I've nothing for the railroad journey.

AUNT MARCH. Of course not, of course not. You're just as bad as he is and then expect me to come to the rescue. You may be willing to end your days in a poorhouse, but I'm not—— *(Almost whining)* I'm a sick, old woman, and I need all I've got. *(Rubbing knees.)*

MRS. MARCH. The money will be repaid, Aunt March.

(READY SLEIGH BELLS.

AUNT MARCH. *(Snaps it at her.)* Humph! But when, I'd like to know? Such wastefulness *(Turns to* MEG.*)*, gallivanting off to Washington on a scare telegram. I can't afford such trips. *(Turns, goes to C., a little tearfully)* When you see my nephew, ask him what he means by going to the war, getting sick and then asking me to pull him out of the hole,

(Stamps her foot and wrenches her knee, rubs it hard and groans.) What does he mean by it, I say, what does he mean? Oh, oh! My knee! Why don't you ask me to sit down? *(Mrs. March offers her chair R. of table. Aunt March refuses. Aunt March drops into chair L. of table C.)* Where's Josephine? She's the only practical one in this family.

Meg. Jo went out to do some errands for Mother. Laurie——

Aunt March. *(Interrupting.)* Just as I thought. She is probably gadding about with that rattle-pated boy. It's not proper.

Mrs. March. *(Quietly)* Jo—*(Pause.)*—is not with Laurie, Aunt March.

Aunt March. So much the better. Oh, my knee. *(Bus. of rubbing left knee, sees her mistake—shifts hand quickly to right knee. Looks covertly to see if Mrs. March or Meg notices this.)* My knee! I'll never sleep to-night. *(Rises.)* Tell Josephine to come and read to me. *(Goes to door, Meg following anxiously.)* I hope for good news of my nephew, but don't expect it. March never had much stamina. Good night. Ah! *(Feeling in her reticule and handing a roll of bills and a check to Meg)* Here's the twenty-five you asked for, and a check for fifty more. Oh, I know there are plenty of bills to pay.

(Ad lib exit, slamming door behind her so suddenly, that neither Mrs. March or Meg have the chance to say good night or thank you.)

(Sleighbells, Meg drops and kisses her mother—giving her the money.)

Meg. Oh, Marmee! I was afraid she wasn't going to give it to you after all! *(Goes to fireplace, pokes fire.)*

Mrs. March. *(Sits* r. *of table.)* I was sure she would, Meg. She has a kind heart, but is ashamed to show it.

*(*Beth *and* Amy *come creeping down the stairs, after peeking over the railing to see if* Aunt March *is gone.* Beth *has brooch,* Amy *her mother's bonnet and shawl and bag. The late afternoon light has been slowly fading during the* Aunt March *interview.* Mrs. March *has seated herself* r. *of table* c. Beth *comes* r. *of her mother,* Amy l.*)*

Beth. Marmee!
Amy. Marmee, we were afraid to come down. She was a raging Vulcan.
Meg. *(At fireplace, laughing, in spite of her anxiety)* Oh, Amy, if you mean a volcano, why don't you say so?
Beth. She was kind about the money, though. *(Hands* Mrs. March *an old-fashioned hair brooch.)* Here's your brooch with Father's hair in it, Marmee. I thought you'd want to wear it.
Mrs. March. *(With emotion, pinning on the brooch)* Thank you, dearie. *(*Meg *goes to back of table* c.*)*
Beth. *(Sound of someone stamping feet in hall)* That must be Jo. Lucky she missed Aunt March

(Enter Jo, *hurriedly, looking blown about and dis-heveled, snow on hat and cape.)*

Jo. Saw Aunt March come out, so I **dodged** through the garden. I knew she wouldn't **give us** anything but advice, and from her face, I guess you got that in large doses. Well, we're independent of her, at any rate, Marmee, and—— *(Putting roll of bills in her mother's lap.)* here's my contribution toward making Father comfortable and bringing him home.

MRS. MARCH. My dear! Where did you get it? Twenty-five dollars! Jo, dear, I hope you haven't done anything rash?

JO. No, it's mine honestly. (*L. of table* C., *takes off mittens and cape, throws them on chair* L. *of table* C.) I didn't beg, borrow or steal it, I only sold what was my own.

(Takes off her hat, showing her hair bobbed short, like a boy's. General outcry from all.)

(READY SLEIGH BELLS.

MRS. MARCH. Your hair, your beautiful hair!

(Puts out her arms. Jo goes and drops on her knees. Head on mother's lap. MRS. MARCH kisses the shorn head.)

MEG. (*Back of table* C.) Oh, Jo, how could you!

AMY. (*Back of table* C.) Your one beauty!

MRS. MARCH. (*Very tenderly*) My dear. (*Raising Jo's face and kissing her*) There was no need of this.

BETH. (R. *of* MARMEE.) She doesn't look like my Jo any more, but—(*Hugging her and crying at the same time.*)—I love her dearly for it.

JO. (*Rumpling up her hair.*) It doesn't affect the fate of the nation, so don't wail about it, Beth. It will be good for my vanity. I was getting proud of my mop. Besides, it will cool my brain. I'm sat-isfied.

(BETH rises, goes up stage back of MARMEE. AMY comforts her.)

Mrs. March. But I am not, Jo. I know how willingly you sacrificed your vanity, as you call it, for your love; but, my dear, it wasn't necessary. Aunt March has helped us—— *(Jo sits back, disappointed)* And I'm afraid you'll regret it one of these days.

Jo. Oh, no, I won't. *(Rises, goes l.c.)*

Meg. What made you do it?

Jo. Well, I was wild to do something for Father, and I'd have sold the nose off my face for him, if anybody would have bought it. I've seen tails of hair, marked $40, not nearly as thick as mine. It was the only thing I had to sell, so I dashed into the shop and asked what they would give for it.

Beth. I don't see how you dared!

(SLEIGH BELLS OFF l.)

Jo. Oh, he was a little man, who looked as if he only lived to oil his hair. He hesitated a little bit. I told him in my topsy-turvy way what I wanted the money for. His wife said, "Take it, Thomas, and oblige the young lady."

Amy. Didn't you feel dreadfully when the first cut came?

Jo. Well, I did feel queer when I saw the dear old hair laid out on the table.

Laurie. All ready?

(As he enters, followed almost immediately by Mr. Laurence and Mr. Brooke.)

Laurie. *(l.c. Catching sight of Jo's shorn head)* Jo, what the dickens have you done? Are you trying to make a porcupine of yourself? You look like——

(Jo turns up l.c. Meg puts arm around her.)

MEG. *(Interrupting, speaking directly to* LAU-
RIE*)* Hush, Laurie, don't say anything now.

MR. LAURENCE. *(L.)* Time to go, Madam. The
conveyance is here.

(The GIRLS *gather around* MRS. MARCH. BETH R.,
puts her bonnet on, then pulls the strings out.
MEG *puts on* R. *overshoe.* JO *pulls on her* L.
overshoe and AMY *puts on her shawl.)*

MRS. MARCH. *(*HANNAH *drags in small hair
cloth trunk.* BROOKE *and* LAURIE *go up* R., *take
trunk and exit* L.I. MR. LAURENCE *stands at door
looking at his watch.)* Children, I leave you to Hannah's care and Mr. Laurence's protection. Don't
grieve and fret, but go on with your work as usual.
(Rises.) Hope and keep busy. Remember that you
can never be fatherless. *(Moving toward door* L.I.
Kissing MEG R.*)* Meg, dear, be prudent, watch over
your sisters. *(Kissing* JO L.*)* Be patient, Jo, don't
do anything rash or get despondent. *(Kissing* BETH
L.*)* Comfort yourself with your music, deary.
(Kissing AMY.*)* Amy, help all you can and be
obedient.

*(*MRS. MARCH *puts left arm around Beth, upstage,
and right around* AMY *downstage—*MEG *and*
JO *follow behind.)*

ALL. We will, Marmee, don't fret about us.
(Ad lib, as they go to door L.*)*

SLEIGH BELLS SLOWLY DIE AWAY.)

(Exit all but JO, *who goes to window* C. *and stands
there waving as the sleigh bells die away.)*

MRS. MARCH. *(Outside, as sleigh bells start)*
God bless you, dearies.

(As MEG *returns, goes* C. BETH *and* AMY *enter and stand at the door* L.I. JO *comes slowly down-stage* R.C. *She gives a little sob.)*

MEG. *(Tenderly)* Jo, dear, what is it?

JO. *(Trying to stifle her emotions)* I was just having a little private moan, that's all.

MEG. Are you crying about Father?

JO. No, not now.

MEG. What then?

JO. *(This time a full-fledged wail)* It's—it's—my—my hair! *(Kneels beside chair* R. *of table* C. MEG *comforts her, leans over her in sympathy.)*

HANNAH. *(As the slow curtain begins to come down,* HANNAH *appears in the dining-room door, her eyes red from weeping, sniffling and trying to get hold of herself)* Will yez have hash or fish-balls for breakfast, gurruls?

QUICK CURTAIN

(Second curtain. HANNAH *off.* BETH *kneeling at fireplace hugging* MARMEE'S *slippers.* MEG *in chair* R. *of* C. *table, with her arm around* JO.' AMY *at door* L *Third curtain—line up of* MEG, JO, BETH *and* AMY—*curtsey.)*

ACT TWO

Scene One: *Same as Act One.*
Time: *Three months later. Morning. March, 1864.*
Music at Rise: *CURTAIN UP; "The Birds of Aberfeldy."*
Lights Full-up: *No change. Medium curtain.*
Discovered: Mrs. March *seated* l. *of table* c., *turned toward fireplace a little, sewing. Enter* Laurie, l.i., *slips down back of her, puts two or three flowers in a slender vase beside her and gives her a hearty kiss and hug. Wing chair at fireplace removed—a small upholstered settee replaces it.*

Laurie. Good morning, Madam Mother!

Mrs. March. Oh, Laurie!

Laurie. What report from Mr. March and Beth?

Mrs. March. Both are better, I am happy to say. And it's good to have him home again. You never forget my nosegay, Laurie.

Laurie. *(Goes* l.c.*)* Where's Jo? I've something to tell her.

Mrs. March. *(Putting down her sewing and rising)* I'll send her to you, dear. She's playing nurse to Father and Beth in the study. *(Goes from room to study door* r.i.e. *Takes vase of flowers with her.)*

48

LAURIE. Tell her I've a plummy bit of news.

(MRS. MARCH laughs and exits L.C. LAURIE walks up and down the room L., hands in pockets, singing "How Can I Bear to Leave Thee?" Gazes out of window L. with hands clasped burlesque lover style, sings to second line, when Jo enters—LAURIE laughs.)

JO. *(Enters R.I.E., carries her little old-fashioned writing box under her arm. Goes to front of table C.)* What's your secret, Teddy?

LAURIE. *(Comes C.)* Well, I may get into a scrape for telling it, and I never feel easy in my mind till I've told you any plummy news I get.

JO. Out with it—is it nice?

LAURIE. Oh, it's spandy nice!

JO. Well, fire away then!

LAURIE. *(In front of table C.)* I know where Meg's glove is.

JO. *(In front of table C.—disappointed)* Is that all?

LAURIE. It's quite enough for the present, as you'll agree when I tell you where.

JO. Tell then——

LAURIE. *(Bends down and whispers in Jo's ear)* John Brooke has it.

JO. John Brooke has it—how do you know? *(Breaks away to R.)*

LAURIE. Saw it.

JO. Where?

LAURIE. Pocket. I asked him if he'd popped the question and he owned up he was afraid to. He's so poor and she's so young. Isn't it romantic?

JO. *(Goes L.C.)* No, it's horrid.

LAURIE. I thought you'd be pleased.

JO. At the thought of anyone coming to take Meg away? No, thank you.

LAURIE. *(Meaningly, sitting against* c. *table)* You'll feel better about it when someone comes to take you away.

Jo. Like to see anyone try it—— *(With clenched fists.)*

LAURIE. *(*c.*, chuckling)* So should I.

Jo. *(Rumpling her hair fretfully)* Secrets don't agree with me, Teddy. I feel rumpled in my mind.

LAURIE. *(Soothingly, goes to* Jo, L.C.*)* Amy and I are going skating by-and-by. Come along and forget your troubles.

Jo. Can't—want to finish a story. *(Goes to table, sits* L. *of it.)*

LAURIE. Such ambition! Oh, come along with Amy and me.

Jo. *(Picking up her quill pen—snaps out)* Go away, Teddy. I'm busy.

LAURIE. Ouch! All right—*(Starting toward hall door)*—but this will be about the last day for the river. *(Exits* L.I.*)* ·

*(*Jo, *busy with her papers and evidently furious at what she has heard, jumps up from her chair, dashes her quill pen down on the table, throws a book violently to the floor. Enter* MRS. MARCH *unseen* R.I.*)*

Jo. Oh, I'm so cross—I wish I'd never been born. *(Buries her head in her hands as she sits by table.)*

MRS. MARCH. *(Goes over quietly, back of table, and taking the tumbled head in her arms, at back of* Jo*)* Why, Jo, what is it?

Jo. Oh, it's my dreadful temper, Marmee. I get so savage when I'm in a passion, I could hurt anyone and enjoy it. Oh, Mother, help me, help me! *(Arms around* MARMEE'S *waist)*

Mrs. March.   Jo, dear, you think your temper is
the worst in the world—*(Jo nods)*—but mine's just
like it.

Jo.   Yours, Mother?   Why, you're never angry.

Mrs. March.   My dear, I have been trying to
cure it for forty years and have only succeeded in
controlling it. *(Starts, picks up quill pen* r.c.*)*   I
still have to learn not to feel it—*(Smiling)*—though
that may take me another forty years. *(Sits down,
bringing chair forward a little, takes up work basket,* r. *of table* c.*)*   What's the trouble?

Jo. *(Rising)*   I want to tell you something,
Mother.

Mrs. March.   About Meg?

Jo.   How quickly you guessed.   Although it's a
little thing, it fidgets me.

Mrs. March.   Well, tell me all about it.

Jo. *(Flops down on the floor in front of table
at her mother's feet)*   Well, Meg left a pair of
gloves over at the Laurences' and only one was returned.   We forgot all about it, till *Teddy* told me
that *Mr. Brooke* has it.

Mrs. March. *(Quickly)*   How could Laurie
know that?

Jo.   *Mr. Brooke* kept it in his pocket, and once
it fell out and Teddy joked him about it.   *Mr.
Brooke* owned that he *liked Meg.*   Now, isn't that a
dreadful state of things?

Mrs. March.   Do you think Meg cares for him?

Jo.   Mercy me!   I don't know anything about
love and such nonsense.   In novels the girls show it
by starting and blushing, fainting away, and acting
like fools.   Now Meg doesn't do anything of the
sort; she eats and drinks and sleeps like a sensible
creature.

Mrs. March.   Then you fancy that Meg is *not*
interested in John?

Jo. *(Astonished)*   *Who?*

MRS. MARCH. Mr. Brooke. *(Jo starts to rise with a groan)* We fell into the way of calling him John at the hospital.

JO. *(Rising to feet and striding up and down L.C.)* Oh, dear, I know you'll take his part. He's been good to Father, so you'll let Meg marry him, if she wants to. O-o-oh, the mean thing! To go petting Papa just to wheedle *you. (Kicks newel post.)*

MRS. MARCH. My dear, don't get angry. John was so devoted to poor Father, we couldn't help getting fond of him.

JO. But that's no reason why he should try to *steal* Meg.

MRS. MARCH. He was perfectly open and honorable about Meg. He told us he loved her and only asked the right to try to make her love him.

JO. *(Still angry)* In my opinion, he tried first and asked leave second. *(Comes downstage a little, shaking her fist at window L.)* Oh, I knew there was mischief brewing. I just wish I could marry Meg myself and keep her safe in the family.

MRS. MARCH. *(Smiling)* Jo, say nothing to Meg about this, please. Perhaps she does not care for him.

JO. *(L.C.)* Oh, I don't know. She likes *brown* eyes and doesn't think *John* an ugly name. *(Gives a funny little nod of head)*

MRS. MARCH. *(Smiling in spite of herself)* Not very fatal symptoms, Jo.

JO. *(Pathetically)* Well, I feel it in the air, Marmee. They'll go lovering about the house and we shall have to dodge. *(Goes up to desk L.)*

MRS. MARCH. My dear, John has his way to make in the world. He's in no position to marry now.

JO. Oh, he'll scratch up a fortune somewhere and carry her off and make a hole in the family, and

I shall break my heart and be abominally uncomfortable. *(Comes down)* Oh, dear me, why weren't we all boys? Then there wouldn't be any bother.

(Mrs. March sighs—bus.)

Jo. *(Comes down to her—in front of table)* You don't like it either, Mother. Let's send him about his business, and all be happy together as we always have been.

Mrs. March. I did wrong to sigh, Jo. It is natural and right that you should all go to homes of your own in time, but I want to keep my girls with me as long as I can, and I am sorry this happened so soon.

Jo. So am I, and I'm disappointed about Meg, for I had planned to have her marry Teddy by-and-by, and sit in the lap of luxury all her days.

Mrs. March. Money is a needful and precious thing, and many times a beautiful thing, but I'd rather see my girls poor men's wives if they were happy and contented, than queens on thrones without self-respect and peace. *(Places hand over Jo's on table)* Let time and their own hearts mate our friends, Jo. Don't make plans, lest they spoil our friendships.

Jo. Well, I won't, but I hate to see things going all criss-cross and getting snarled up, when a pull here and a snip there would straighten it out. *(Mr. March enters, looks back into study, smiling to Beth, turns as he hears "flatirons" and "cats." Jo picks up her book and quill pen she had thrown to floor.)* I wish wearing flatirons on our heads would keep us from growing up. But buds will be roses, and kittens, cats, more's the pity. *(Sits L. of table.)*

March. *(Comes to R.C.)* Beth has awakened, Mother. What's that I hear about flatirons and cats, Jo?

*(Goes up to small table at fireplace and gets apple
    and knife. MRS. MARCH goes to door R.I.)*

JO. Only one of my stupid speeches, Father.
AMY. *(Comes downstairs, dressed for skating,
skates over arm.)* I'm going skating with Laurie,
Marmee. We'll stop at the office, Father, for the
mail.

(MARCH goes down to chair R. of table C.)

MRS. MARCH. *(At study door.)* Don't be late
for dinner, Amy.
AMY. *(At door L.I.)* No, Marmee. You know
I am always "punctiluous."

*(MARCH and MRS. MARCH look at each other and
    smile at AMY's attempt at big words. Exit
    AMY hall door L.I. MRS. MARCH study door
    R.I. JO wipes quill on hair and dress.)*

MARCH. *(Smiles, sinking into large chair R. of
table.)* How goes the writing, my daughter? *(Peeling apple.)*
JO. *(Fingering the pen as she speaks)* Oh,
Father—sometimes I get discouraged, tear up pages
and pages, and sometimes—*(Laughing)*—genius
burns. I've been doing a lot of short stories and I
wish I could sell some of 'em. I *do* want to make
some money.
MARCH. *(Stops peeling apple.)* Money isn't the
only thing in the world, my child. *(Places his left
hand on table towards JO.)*
JO. *I know, Plato.* *(She reaches over and pats
his hand.)*
MARCH. *(Smiles, starts peeling apple again)*
Is Aunt March as trying and amusing as ever?
JO. *(Laughing)* She gets worse and worse; and
funnier and funnier.

MARCH. What is the latest wrinkle? *(Laughing)*

JO. Oh, nothing new—washing the poodle, hearing the parrot swear and reading Belsham's Essays. Father, when I think of the good times she might have and doesn't, I don't envy her with all her money.

MARCH. *(Heartily)* You are right, Jo; but you've Uncle March's library to browse in, that's some comfort.

JO. That reminds me, Father; such an interesting man has been there—a Professor Friederich Bhaer.

MARCH. *(Animated)* Oh, the Professor Bhaer who translated Shakespeare into German and is making an English translation of Schiller? *(Puts apple peeling on small piece of paper on table.)*

JO. I had no idea that my middle-aged professor was a celebrity.

MARCH. Neither is he. When his sister was dying he gave up his career and came over here to take care of his two little orphan nephews, whom he is educating in this country.

JO. Why doesn't he educate them in Germany?

MARCH. Their father was an American and it was their mother's last request that her sons be brought up as Americans. So Professor Bhaer adopted not only the boys, but their country, as his own.

JO. A fine, manly thing to do!

MARCH. What is he like?

JO. He isn't handsome, and while he was looking over the books, he was humming like a big bumblebee. Rather stout, a bushy beard, a good nose, and the kindest eyes I ever saw. He looks like a gentleman, even if he has two buttons off his coat and a patch on one shoe.

MR. LAURENCE. *(Enters L.I.)* Good morning, sir.

(Jo rises, meets him, takes his hat and puts it on chair below desk L.; goes back and places chair L. of table C. for LAURENCE.)

MARCH. *(Rising)* Good morning, Mr. Laurence.

LAURENCE. And how are you feeling to-day?

MARCH. *(Smiles, taking paper with apple peeling and goes to fireplace.)* Improving steadily, thank you. Home was what I needed. *(Throws peeling into fireplace.)*

MR. LAURENCE. *(Sits.)* And my little friend Beth?

(Jo sits back of table C.)

MARCH. *(Coming back.)* She is better this morning *(Pauses R.C.)*, though she seems very frail. But I am sure she will gain with the coming of the Spring. *(Coming back to chair R. of table, sits, eating apple.)*

MR. LAURENCE. Miss Jo, have you seen that harum-scarum grandson of mine? What mischief is he up to now?

JO. He's out skating with Amy, sir. Don't worry about Teddy, Mr. Laurence; he'll turn out all right.

MR. LAURENCE. Well, he ought to, after all the kindness you show him over here.

JO. *(Quaintly)* Well, Marmee has always told us: Cast your bread upon the waters, and after many days it will come back—*Buttered!* *(ALL laugh)*

MR. LAURENCE. *(Smiling)* Don't spoil the lad.

(Rises.   Enter BETH, MRS. MARCH *and* MEG.
BETH *thin and pale, showing that she has been
ill. Bus. of settling her comfortably on settee.*
MEG *comes in first,* BETH *second,* MRS. MARCH
third. MEG *and* MRS. MARCH *carry an extra
pillow and afghan for* BETH *to help make her
comfortable.* MRS. MARCH *goes up to settee,
fixing shawl, etc., for* BETH.*)*

MEG. Mr. Laurence, you see that Beth comes
with a royal retinue. *(Goes to settee at fireplace,
helping* MRS. MARCH *fix same.)*
MR. LAURENCE. *(Goes to* BETH R.C.*)* As she
should, our little household queen.
BETH. *(Holds out her hand,* MR. LAURENCE
*kisses it—*BETH *smiles up at him as he bends over
her)* How sunny the days are growing.

*(*JO *goes to desk* L. *carrying her writing box.* MEG
gets picture book out of closet under niche for
BETH. BETH *has bright yarns—and a big spool
with pins making yarn reins which will event-
ually be coiled into a lamp mat.)*

MR. LAURENCE. We must soon get you out
into the sunshine, my child. There is health and
vigor in this air.
MRS. MARCH. Sit here, Mr. Laurence. Beth
always looks forward to her morning visit with you,
sir. *(Goes back to table)*
MR. LAURENCE. *(Sitting.)* Thank you, Madam.

*(*LAURENCE *sits* L. *of* BETH *on settee by fireplace,
talking to her inaudibly, showing her picture
book.* MRS. MARCH *pats* MR. MARCH's *head
tenderly and then sits back of table* C. *and begins sewing.* MR. MARCH *sits quietly, his head
back, eyes closed, as if resting.)*

MEG. *(Goes up to window* C., **stands looking out.**) Here come Amy and Laurie racing along like two children. They are getting too old for such frolics. *(Goes to desk* L.)

JO. *(Sitting in chair at desk* L.—*sadly)* Don't try to make them grow up before their time, Meg. It's hard enough to have you change, all of a sudden.

(Enter LAURIE *and* AMY, *both laughing outside as they come running up, skates over arms.)*

LAURIE. *(Waving a newspaper jubilantly)* Hurrah! Hurrah! Here's a plummy bit of news, and the real sensation of the season. *(Goes to* C. *upstage, back of table a little* L.)

ALL. Oh, what is it?

LAURIE. *(Waving paper triumphantly)* We've a genius in the March family.

*(*BETH *and* MR. LAURENCE *rise and drop down* R.C. MR. LAURENCE *sits on* BETH'S *little stool, takes* BETH *on his knee.)*

MEG. *(Comes* L.C.) I'm sure it's dear old Jo.

LAURIE. (C. *of table* C., *still waving paper)* Be it known by these present that this paper——

JO. *(Goes to* LAURIE, *trying to take paper from him)* The *Spread Eagle.* Oh, Teddy—it isn't—it isn't——

*(*MEG *drops down to* AMY L.)*

LAURIE. *(*C.) It very much is, thank you, a story with a pleasing illustration of a lunatic, a corpse, a villain and a viper. And your name at the bottom, Miss Josephine March. Hurrah for the *Spread Eagle* and the celebrated American authoress.

(Gives Jo *the paper, tossing his skating cap in the air, goes up stage.)*

Jo.   Marmee—Marmee—my story's printed——
(Sits in chair L. *of table, putting paper over face and rocking back and forth)*
LAURIE.   Isn't it fine to see it all in print, and aren't we proud? *(Goes* L.*)*
MARCH.   Let me see, my daughter.

*(*Jo *hands him the paper, which he reads, putting on spectacles.)*

BETH.   *(Holding out her hand,* Jo *goes over to her chair and takes it tenderly)* I knew it—I knew it—oh, my Jo, I am so proud!
AMY.   *(*L. *Dancing about excitedly)* Tell us all about it.   Did Father know or Mother?
MEG.   *(*L.C.*)* How did you ever dare try?
AMY.   How much did you get for it?
Jo.   *(Coming* R.C.*)* Stop jabbering, girls, and I'll tell you all about it.   To begin with, Laurie had read my stuff and he said——
LAURIE.   *(Down* L. *cor., interrupting—*MEG *and* AMY *turn to each one as* Jo *and* LAURIE *interrupt each other)* I said her stories were works of Shakespeare compared to most of the rubbish that is published every day.
Jo.   So I gave him three stories to take to a publisher he knows, and——
LAURIE.   *(Again interrupting)* This is the result.   Two stories accepted, and the third also, if you will cut out the moral.
MR. *and* MRS. MARCH.   Oh, Laurie!
LAURIE.   People don't want to be preached at; morals don't pay nowadays and here's a check for $50. *(Goes to* Jo *in front of table* C., *takes check*

from pocket and hands it to her. MEG *and* AMY *down* L.)

JO. *(In front of table* C., *grabbing check and staring at it as if she doubted her eyes)* $50—ha, ha—and I can write reams of 'em! I can't do much with my hands, but I'll make a battering ram of my head and beat a living out of this topsy-turvy world! *(Turns around to* MRS. MARCH— *tears as* MRS. MARCH *kisses her, back of table* C.)

MARCH. *(Indicating story)* It is good, my daughter, but you can do better than this. "Hitch your wagon to a star," remember, and never mind the money.

AMY. *(Down* L.) I think the money is the nicest part of it. Fancy earning $50 all by yourself. What ever will you do with such a fortune?

JO. *(*L. *of table* C.) Send Beth and Mother to the seashore.

BETH. *(Clapping her hands)* Oh, how splendid! Jo, I can't do it, dear; it would be so selfish!

JO. Oh, but you shall go. I've set my heart on it. That is what I tried for and why I succeeded. I never get on when I think of myself alone, so it will help me to work for you, don't you see?

MEG. Marmee needs to go after nursing two invalids, and she won't leave without you, Beth.

MRS. MARCH. *(Goes to* BETH R.) Beth, dear, let Jo spend her first $50 in her own way.

BETH. It's such a beautiful way. Just like my Jo!

MRS. MARCH. We all want to hear Jo's story, I know. Father, are you too tired to read it aloud? *(Goes* R.C.)

MARCH. *(Rises.)* I never have a chance to get tired, with such devoted nurses. *(Taking them all in—goes* R.) Suppose we go to the study, where the light is better?

(Exits into study R.L. BETH *and* MRS. MARCH *exit after him.* AMY *takes skates and hood up to closet.* MR. LAURENCE *goes to* JO, C., *offering hand.)*

MR. LAURENCE. My sincerest congratulations, Miss Jo.

JO. Thank you, sir. *(Shakes hands with a slap and a grip which* MR. LAURENCE *registers comically)*

MR. LAURENCE. *(Goes to* R.I.E., *bows grandly to* AMY*)* You first, my lady.

*(*AMY *exits* R.I.—LAURENCE *follows.* ALL *heard talking in library a few seconds—"Sit down here,* MR. LAURENCE," *etc., until the door closes.)*

LAURIE. *(Goes* L. *to door)* I must run across with these letters for old Brooke. Oh, Meg, have you seen him since he came home? *(Teasingly.)*

MEG. *(Above desk* L. *with dignity, while* JO *shakes her head at* LAURIE*)* Certainly. He comes to see Father and Mother every day.

LAURIE. *(Laughing and refusing to catch* JO's *eye)* Such devotion—to Father and Mother!

(Exits L. *As the door slams,* MEG *walks to window* L. *and looks out.)*

JO. *(Gazing at the check, smiling happily, to herself as much as to* MEG*)* Why, I can go on spinning yarns like a spider—and perhaps take care of them all.

(Laugh from MEG *makes her look at her;* JO *front of table.)*

MEG. Jo, what is Laurie doing there out in the snow? See, he's on one knee, with his hands clasped looking at me. Now he's pretending to wring tears out of his handkerchief. *(Laughing)* What does the goose mean?

Jo. *(Scornfully)* He's showing you how your John will go on by-and-by. Touching, isn't it?

MEG. *(Comes down to* Jo.*)* Don't say "my John," it isn't proper or true. Please don't plague me, Jo. I've told you I don't care *much* for him, so let us all be friendly and go on as before. *(Goes to desk and takes up sewing)*

Jo. Well, I wish it was settled. I hate to wait, so if you ever intend to do it, make haste and have it over quickly.

MEG. I can't say or do anything till he speaks, and he won't, because Father says I am too young.

Jo. If he did speak, you wouldn't know what to say.

MEG. I'm not so silly and weak as you think! I know just what I'd say—for I've planned it all.

Jo. *(Leaning against table* L. *side)* You've planned it?

MEG. Well, there's no telling what may happen and I wish to be prepared.

Jo. *(Smiling sarcastically)* Would you mind telling me what you'd say?

MEG. Not at all. You are quite old enough to be my confidante, and my experience will be useful to you by-and-by, in your own affairs of this sort.

Jo. *(Facing front)* Don't mean to have any. It's fun to watch other people philander, but I should feel like a fool doing it myself.

MEG. *(Dropping her work and looking dreamily out of window)* I think not, if you liked him very much—and he liked you.

Jo. Humph! I'd rather be an old maid and paddle my own canoe. *(Bluntly, turning to* MEG*)* Well, I thought you were going to tell me your speech to that man.

MEG. Oh, I should merely say, quite calmly and decidedly—— *(Puts down sewing, folds hands in lap—feet together—sits very primly)* "Thank you, Mr. Brooke, you are very kind, but I agree with father that I am too young to enter into any engagement at present. So please say no more, but let us be friends, as we were." *(Settles herself and looks at* Jo.*)*

Jo. *(Looks at* MEG*)* Hum! That's stiff and cool enough. I don't believe you'll ever say it—and if he goes on like the rejected lovers in books, you'll give in.

MEG. *(Rises, goes up to foot of stairs)* No, I won't. I shall tell him I've made up my mind, and shall walk out of the room with dignity. *(Walks as if rehearsing her dignified exit—as she gets to foot of stairs. Knock is heard in the hall)*

BROOKE. *(In hall)* Anybody home?

*(*MEG *flies back to her seat at desk* L. *with a little cry and begins sewing violently.)*

Jo. *(Laughs sarcastically)* Ha, ha! *(Goes, jerks open door and stands in doorway, stopping* BROOKE*)*

BROOKE. *(Enters, startled by the suddenness, raises his hat, looks confused)* Good morning, I came to get my—*(Pause)*—umbrella. That is, to see how your Father finds himself to-day?

Jo. *(Very sarcastic)* It's very well, he's in the rack—I'll get him and tell it you are here.

(Dashes upstairs—stamping. BROOKE *closes door and goes* R.C., *doesn't see* MEG.*)*

MEG. Mother will like to see you. Pray sit down. I'll call her. *(Goes toward* R.*)*

BROOKE. Don't :o. Are you afraid of me, Margaret? *(Stopping her* R.C.*)*

MEG. *(Putting out her hand confidingly at end of speech)* How can I be afraid when you have been so kind to father? I only wish I could thank you for it.

BROOKE. *(Taking her hand in both of his)* Shall I tell you how?

MEG. *(Trying to withdraw her hand, turning her head away)* Oh, no, please don't—I'd rather not.

BROOKE. I only want to know if you care for me a little, Meg. I love you so much, dear.

MEG. *(Hanging her head and speaking abruptly, almost in tears)* I—I don't know.

BROOKE. Will you try to find out? I want to know so much, for I can't go to work with any heart until I know whether I am to have my reward or not.

MEG. *(Falteringly)*, I'm—I'm too young.

BROOKE. I'll wait. And in the meantime, you could be learning to like me. Would it be a very hard lesson, dear?

MEG. Not if I choose to learn.

BROOKE. Please choose to learn. I love to teach and this is easier than Italian.

MEG. *(Looking up, sees that he is smiling— draws away her hand, petulantly)* I don't choose. Please go away and let me be. *(Goes to desk)*

BROOKE. *(Following her anxiously as she walks away)* Do you really mean that?

MEG. Yes, I do. I don't want to be worried about such things. Father says I needn't. It's too soon and I'd rather not!

BROOKE. May I hope you'll change your mind by-and-by?

AUNT MARCH. *(Heard thumping her cane in hall)* Anybody home? Where is everybody?

(Cane thumping. MEG *rushes* BROOKE *off into dining room;* BROOKE *grabbing up his hat by centre table as he goes.* AUNT MARCH *enters* L.I., *stops* L.C. *in time to see* BROOKE *disappearing—*MEG *looks confused and conscious)* Bless me, what's all this? *(Rapping her cane and glaring fiercely at* MEG *and at dining-room door)*

MEG. It's father's friend. I'm so surprised to see you. *(Fixes chair* L. *of table for* AUNT MARCH*)*

AUNT MARCH. *(Grimly)* That's evident. What's father's friend been saying to make you look like a "Piny"? *(Starts to cross)* There's mischief going on here and I insist upon knowing what it is. *(Goes to chair* R. *of table and sits—another tap of cane)*

MEG. *(*L. *of table)* We were merely talking. Mr. Brooke came for—for his umbrella.

AUNT MARCH. Brooke? That boys' tutor? Ah, I understand now. You haven't gone and accepted him, child?

MEG. Hush, he'll hear! Sha'n't I call Mother?

AUNT MARCH. Not yet. Tell me, do you mean to marry this Cook?

MEG. Brooke.

AUNT MARCH. If you do, not one penny of my money goes to you. Remember that.

MEG. *(Standing* L. *of table, and facing the old lady, speaking with unwonted spirit)* I shall marry whom I please, Aunt March, and you can leave your money to anyone you like.

AUNT MARCH. *(Tapping her cane and facing front)* Hoighty-toity! *(*LAURIE *enters, unseen by either* MEG *or* AUNT MARCH, *sees there is trouble, goes up the stairs in about two or three bounds, turns at door and gives mock bow—exits)* Is that the way you take my advice, Miss? You'll be sorry for it by and by, when you've tried love in a cottage and found it a failure.

MEG. *(Still ruffled)* It can't be worse than some people find it in big houses.

AUNT MARCH. *(Putting on her glasses and tak ing a long look at* MEG *before she speaks)* Now, Meg, my dear, be reasonable and take my advice I don't want you to spoil your whole life by making a mistake in the beginning. You ought to marry well and help your family. It's your duty to make a rich match, and it ought to be impressed upon you.

MEG. Father and Mother don't think so. They like John, though he is poor.

AUNT MARCH. Your parents, my dear, have no more worldly wisdom than two babies.

MEG. I'm glad of it.

(FLASH ORCH.)

AUNT MARCH. This Crooke——

MEG. Brooke!

AUNT MARCH. Is poor, and hasn't got any rich relatives, has he?

MEG. No, but he has many warm friends.

AUNT MARCH. *(Snappishly)* You can't live on them. Try it, and see how cool they'll grow. He hasn't any business, has he?

MEG. Not yet, but Mr. Laurence is going to help him.

AUNT MARCH. Huh, that won't last long. So you intend to marry a man without money, position or business, and go on working harder than you do now, when you might be comfortable all your days by minding me and doing better. I thought you had more sense, Meg.

(WARN)

MEG. *(Realizing by this time how much she loves* BROOKE*)* I couldn't do better if I waited half my life. John is good and wise. He has heaps of talent,—he's willing to work and sure to get on, he's so energetic and brave. And I'm proud to think he cares for me, though I am young and silly.

AUNT MARCH. He knows you've got rich relations, child.

MEG. *(Stamping her foot and speaking rapidly in her anger)* Aunt March, how dare you say such a thing? John is above such meanness, and I won't listen to you a minute if you talk so. My John wouldn't marry for money any more than I would. I'm not afraid of being poor, for I've been happy so far, and I know I shall be with him, because he loves me and I—I——

AUNT MARCH. *(Rising and going toward door L.I.)* Well, I wash my hands of the whole affair. You are a wilful child and you have lost more than you know by this piece of folly—— *(Movement of MEG toward her)* No, I won't stop! I'm disappointed in you and haven't spirit to see your father now. Don't expect anything from me when you're married. Your Mr. Crooke's friends must take care of you. I'm done with you forever.

(She exits, slamming door behind her. MEG goes upstage by window, almost ready to cry)

BROOKE. *(Enters, crosses to her)* I couldn't help hearing, Meg. Thank you for defending me, and Aunt March for proving that you do care for me a little bit.

MEG. I didn't know how much till she abused you.

BROOKE. Then I needn't go away; but stay and be happy, dear?

MEG. *(Hiding face on BROOKE's shoulder)* Yes, John.

*(He raises her face, kisses her. She gasps, laughs
and ducks under his arm and they sit together
on seat under stairway. Jo appears on staircase with LAURIE in her train—they peek and
listen.)*

Jo. There! she has had it out with Aunt March,
and has sent Brooke away.

*(LAURIE sees MEG and BROOKE, gleefully points to
them, calling Jo's attention. Jo gasps and comes
downstairs flying. BROOKE looks up, he and
MEG rise.)*

BROOKE. Sister Jo, congratulate us! *(Takes
MEG in his arms again and kisses her)*
Jo. *(Gives funny little gasp, rushes to study
door, throws it open and calls out)* Father—Mother
—somebody—come quick! John Brooke is acting
dreadfully—and Meg likes it!

*(LAURIE stands on the stairs laughing and holding
on to his sides—MEG and BROOKE are together
down L.—Jo just turning from study door—
others begin to appear as the*

CURTAIN

*(Curtain right up quick for second curtain. Music—
"Haste to the Wedding"—played very quick
and forte for all curtains.)*

*(SECOND PICTURE: Family all on—Jo right of
C., gasps as JOHN kisses her; tries to rub it off
and dashes out of door L. as family laugh.
LAURIE, seeing, is convulsed, and slides downstairs.)*

(THIRD PICTURE:—Company.)

(FOURTH CURTAIN: Entire company crosses stage from L.I. to R.I. in character with characteristic bow to audience in the c.)

1st.   HANNAH
2nd.   MR. LAURENCE
3rd.   MR. and MRS. MARCH
4th.   BETH
5th.   AMY
6th.   LAURIE
7th.   AUNT MARCH
8th.   MEG and BROOKE
9th.   JO.

END OF SCENE ONE

2 minute wait.

SCENE TWO

SCENE: *Same as Scene One.*
TIME: *Six months later. September, 1864. Late afternoon.*
MUSIC: Curtain up on "Lorelei."

Lights open with Light Amber. Medium curtain.

DISCOVERED: Jo *writing L. of table c., ink blot on nose. She is enveloped in a big black apron and wears a black cap with a flaming red bow on top. Jo, in fits of abstraction, wipes her quill pen upon one or the other, and jabs it almost viciously in the ink. Evidently "Genius is burning," and she is absorbed in her work.*

MEG *sits sewing* R. *of table.* *She is listening to* MARCH'S *voice as he reads aloud in the study* R.I.

MARCH. *(Off)* "The fat boy pointed to the destination of the pies. 'Wery good,' said Sam, 'stick a bit o' Christmas in 'em. There now, we look compact and comfortable, as the father said when he cut his little boy's head off to cure him o' squintin'.'"

(Amid a burst of laughter which follows, HANNAH *enters from dining room and goes to* MEG.*)*

HANNAH. Miss Meg, come quick! Miss Amy's hoppin' around the woodshed with her foot in some white stuff—and she can't git it out.

AMY. *(Comes hopping on from dining room with the pan on her right foot, crying)* I can't get it out—*(Ad lib. Comes to* R.C. Jo *looks up and roars, then goes on with her writing)*

MEG. *(Rises and puts down her work impatiently)* Oh, dear, Amy, I do wish you would leave plaster modeling alone.

HANNAH. Well, she's crazy about them chiny figgers she calls stattys. *(*HANNAH, MEG *and* AMY *exit into dining room her bare leg and the pan stuck out behind—as she hops off* R. 3, *ad lib outside)* I can't pull her foot out of the pan!

MEG. Well, try now, Hannah!

*(*AMY *screams.* Jo, *who has evidently reached the end of her inspiration, rises and stretches herself, casting aside apron and cap on desk* L., *stretches arms over her head; as she yawns and shakes herself, enter* MARCH *and* BETH *from study;* MARCH *with book under his arm;* BETH *with a little basket in her hand.)*

Jo. What—no more Pickwick?

March. *(Laying book on mantel at fireplace, with his back to fire, takes off spectacles and begins cleaning them with handkerchief)* Not for the present. I'm read out.

Beth. *(Goes to* Jo, *up* l. *near desk)* Jo, don't you want to help me cut the sunflowers? We need the seeds to feed Aunt Cockletop and her family of chicks.

*(*Mrs. March *comes down the stairs. She is wearing a little knitted shawl over her shoulders, which she takes off and puts on* Beth.*)*

Jo. I'll be glad of the exercise and—*(Laughing)* the chance to cool my fevered brain. *(Takes off net and shakes down her hair, which falls loosely about her shoulders)* Besides, I've got to wait and fill up my idea box again.

Mrs. March. *(The two girls exit, laughing, hall door.* Mrs. March *takes her work basket from* c. *table and goes over to* March, *sitting on settee at fireplace)* Father, I am worried about Amy and Laurie and Jo.

March. Worried?   You   don't   think   that Amy——?

Mrs. March. Mother's eyes are keen, dear, and there is no question in my mind that Amy cares for Laurie in quite another way than he does for her. He loves her, of course, but it's entirely the big brother attitude.

March. And Jo?

Mrs. March. I've sometimes feared Jo's heart would never be touched with a real romance.

March. *(Thoughtfully)* With her, brain is developing before heart.

Mrs. March. *(Smiling)* Yes; she prefers imaginary heroes to real ones, says that when she gets tired of them she can lock them up in the old tin kitchen where she keeps her manuscripts. And yet——

MARCH. And yet—— (*Sits on settee* R. *of* MRS. MARCH, *putting arm around her*) What else have those keen, motherly eyes discovered?

MRS. MARCH. Do you remember how interested Jo was in that elderly Professor?

MARCH. (*Looks surprised*) Professor Bhaer?

MRS. MARCH. Well, since she's been teaching Mrs. Kirk's children, she has seen him again. He rooms at the Kirks; he's teaching her German, and she sews on his buttons and darns his socks.

MARCH. (*Smiling and shaking his head in a deprecating way, as he taps his wife's cheek gently*) You dear, foolish mother. I shouldn't call darning socks a love symptom. (*Rises*)

MEG. (*Enters downstairs, dressed for walking*) I'm going down to the office to walk up with John, Mother.

MRS. MARCH. Very well, dear; bring John back to tea.

MEG. (*Goes to hall door* L.I.) Thanks, Marmee.

(*Curtseys and exits* L.I.)

Jo. (*Coming in from dining room, her hair tidy again, carrying letter, absorbed and pleased, comes to* R.C., *suddenly becomes aware of presence of father and mother and gives an embarrassed look*) Ha—ha—Marmee, you said I might ask my professor to call and he's coming this afternoon.

(MR. *and* MRS. MARCH *exchange a meaning look, which Jo does not see—being upstage and back of table to chair* L. *Bus. of tucking letter into dress, taking apron and cap from chair and throwing them in closet on floor.* MARCH *shakes his head, and, chuckling to himself, disappears into the study* R.I. *Jo fixes the bow at her neck, comes down to chair* L. *of table* C. *and takes up her pen.)*

MRS. MARCH. *(Takes up her sewing)* You seem very much interested in the professor, Jo.

JO. Well, he advised me to study simple, true characters, so I proceeded to study him. I find him a great puzzle. He's not fascinating or brilliant, and yet people gather about him as naturally as about a genial fire. He's poor, yet he always appears to be giving something away. He's a stranger, yet everyone's his friend. He's plain and peculiar and I've been trying to discover his charm and I've finally decided that it's a benevolence that has worked the miracle. *(With a funny little laugh)* Why, Mother, his very boots are benevolent.

AMY. *(Enters, wearing* MEG'S *dress of Act One made over)* Marmee, may I wear your little pearl pin to the dance to-night? *(Bus. of scratching left ankle with right foot)*

MRS. MARCH. Surely, dear, it is simple enough to be quite appropriate for my little girl.

JO. Where are you going, Amy?

AMY. Aunt Curtis has asked me to dine there to-night, and she will take Flo and me to Mamie Gardner's dance.

MRS. MARCH. What are you going to wear, dear?

AMY. I've covered Flo's old white silk with tarletan, and I shall loop it with rosebuds.

JO. *(Disapprovingly)* Don't see why you want to go to parties, Amy, and truckle to a parcel of girls who don't care a sixpence for you, just because they wear French heels and ride in coupes.

AMY. *(Indignantly)* I don't truckle, and I hate being patronized as much as you do, but I like people and mean to make the most of every chance I get.

JO. Humph! I like luxury, but I prefer independence.

AMY. *(Ruffled at* JO's *insinuation)* Well, *you* can go through the world with your elbows out and your nose in the air and call it independence, if you like. It's not my way.

MRS. MARCH. *(Mildly)* Don't squabble, children. *(*AMY *turns to bay window)* Amy—Amy—*(On second "*AMY*"—*AMY *comes down stage, smiling)* I think you turned Meg's old hat into a really charming creation.

JO. Meg's *old* hat? Isn't it a *new* one?

AMY. *(Triumphantly)* Not at all. It's her old one. I painted it with water colors, and her boots to match.

JO. *(Ashamed of her recent temper, and ready to make amends)* Amy, it certainly is a great comfort to have an "artistic" sister. *(*AMY, *mollified, goes up to window* C., *takes up drawing board)*

*(*MEG *and* BROOKE *laugh outside, then enter, looking radiant.* BROOKE *places hat on chair below desk* L.; MEG *places hat and scarf on seat under stairway.)*

MRS. MARCH. Well, John?

BROOKE. Meg and I have been house-hunting.

*(*JO *glares at him.)*

MRS. MARCH. Isn't it a little soon, John, when the wedding date isn't fixed?

MEG. *(Goes to* R. *of* C. *at back)* We've found such a dear little cottage, Mother—the Dove Cote, John calls it.

Jo. Mush! *(Disgusted, jams elbows on table and her chin in her hands)*

MEG. Will you go with us to see it to-morrow?

MRS. MARCH. Why, of course I will. John, will you stay to tea? *(Rises)*

BROOKE. *(Looks at* Jo, *half-afraid—she glares at him)* Only too glad of the chance, ma'am.

*(*MRS. MARCH *exits to dining room.)*

MEG. *(Sits on settee* L. *side at fireplace with a skein of worsted, which she holds out to* BROOKE*)* John, won't you hold this for me, please?

*(*BROOKE, *without a word, goes to table* C., *to seat himself at fireplace* R.; *he and* MEG *become absorbed in each other.* Jo, *who has taken up a book, looks over at them—*AMY, *sitting at back of table* C., *begins sketching them and nudges* Jo *to make her look at the lovers.)*

Jo. I hate lovering. *(Sounds of a gay whistle outside, she gives a sigh of satisfaction)* Toodles is coming! Now, perhaps, we shall have some sensible conversation.

AMY. I wish you wouldn't call Laurie Toodles, Jo. It isn't dignified.

(Enter LAURIE, *carrying brown parcel; goes over to* MEG *as soon as he spies her and presents it with sweeping bow.)*

Jo. Teddy!

*(*LAURIE *ignores* Jo.)*

LAURIE. For Mrs. John Brooke! *(Places parcel in her lap)*

MEG. Oh, Laurie——

LAURIE. With the maker's compliments and congratulations. Any time, when John is away and you get frightened, Mrs. Meg—*(Takes rattle which MEG has undone)*—just swing this out of the front window, and it will rouse the neighborhood in a jiffy. *(It is a mammoth rattle, and, as LAURIE finishes, he takes it from MEG and gives a sample of its power, that makes them cover their ears—then he hands the rattle back to MEG, who laughs so that she cannot thank him. He falls into an attitude of mock devotion before AMY)* Amy, you are getting altogether too handsome for a single lady. I shall warn grandpa.

(Goes to AMY at back of table c.)

AMY. *(Nettled)* Don't be absurd, Laurie. Will you ever grow up?

LAURIE. I'm doing my best, ma'am—but six feet is about all a man can do in these degenerate days. *(Looks over at BROOKE and MEG, who are again absorbed)* Oh, gaze upon the happy lovers!

AMY. Aren't they radiant? I want to paint Meg in her wedding gown, the first bride in the March family.

(JO, evidently disgusted at the talk about lovers, grabs up her writing desk and goes to desk L., slamming small writing case down on desk L. sits.)

LAURIE. Old Brooke has asked me to the wedding, and I accepted on the spot. Told him I'd come if I were at the end of the earth, for the sight of Jo's face on that occasion would be worth a long journey.

AMY. *(Has risen as he spoke—puts drawing board on small table at back, starts to go upstairs)*

Yes, wouldn't it? I must dress or I shall be late.
(Exits)

LAURIE. *(At newel post L., evidently in teasing mood—looks at* MEG *and* JOHN, *then goes over to* Jo*)* You don't look festive, ma'am, what's the matter?

Jo. I don't approve of the match. You can't know how hard it is for me to give up Meg.

LAURIE. *(Going to her consolingly)* You don't give her up. You only go halves.

Jo. I've lost my dearest friend.

LAURIE. You've got me, anyhow, and I'll stand by you, Jo, all the days of my life. *(Holds out hand)*

Jo. *(Shaking hands with him)* I know you will. You're always such a comfort to me, Teddy.

LAURIE. Well, now, don't be dismal, there's a good fellow. It'll be very jolly to see Mrs. Meg in her own little home; but, oh, I say, Jo, that little Parker is getting desperate about *Amy*.

Jo. *(Aghast)* About Amy?

LAURIE. Yes. He writes poetry about her and all that sort of thing. We'd better nip his little passion in the bud, hadn't we?

Jo. *(Startled)* Of course we had. The idea! We don't want any more marrying in this family for years to come. Mercy on us, what are the children thinking about?

LAURIE. *(Chuckling)* It's a fast age, and I don't know what we are coming to, ma'am. You're a mere infant, but you'll go next, Jo.

Jo. Don't be alarmed. There should always be one old maid in the family—and I'm *it!* *(*LAURIE *laughs—*Jo's *tone changes)* I think it's dreadful to break up families so—— *(Bell rings and* Jo *starts for* L. *door, consciously)* Let's change the subject.

LAURIE. *(Meaningly)* You'll go next.

(MEG and JOHN, hearing bell, quietly exit to study, bus.—MEG dragging him off with yarn. Enter HANNAH, starts to answer door.)

JO. *(With hand on the knob, turns to HANNAH)* I'll open the door, Hannah. Please tell father and mother that the Professor is here.

HANNAH. *(Turning to exit to dining room, sees MRS. MARCH entering from dining room, goes into dining room, speaking as she goes)* Someone to see Miss Jo, ma'am.

(A moment later MARCH, smiling, steps softly out of study, as if leaving field free for the lovers— MR. and MRS. MARCH R.C. LAURIE is up stage a little L.C.)

JO. *(Outside)* Oh, Mr. Bhaer, I am so glad to see you.

BHAER. *(Outside)* And I to see you, Mees Marsche—— *(They reach the doorway together, Jo leading the way)* But no, you haf a party?

(Jo enters first, takes PROFESSOR'S silk hat and puts it on chair L.; BHAER stops just inside room as he sees others.)

JO. No, we haven't—only the family. Come in and make one of us.

(Ready electrician to light small piece of paper in fireplace.)

BHAER. If I should not be Monsieur De Trop, I will gladly see them all.

JO. Father—Mother—this is my friend, Professor Bhaer.

*(*BHAER *goes* C.—MRS. MARCH *goes to him, greets
and shakes hands with him; then* MARCH *goes,
same bus.* MR. MARCH *and* MRS. MARCH *stand*
L. *and* R. *of table* C. *Cordial greeting from all
but* LAURIE, *who stands aloof.* JO, *noting this,
turns to him.)*

BHAER. I am glad to meet you. *(Turning to*
Jo, L.*)* This is your friend of whom you speak?
   Jo. Yes, my boy Teddy. I'm very proud of him.
   LAURIE. *(*L.*)* Oh, come now, Jo, don't speak
as if I were a lap-dog or Beth's kitten. *(Evidently
trying to put aside his annoyance, turns toward*
BHAER, *with his usual charming manner)* I'm glad
to meet you, Professor Bhaer. Please remember
there's always a welcome for you over the way.
(Indicating the LAURENCE *home with a gesture of
his head toward the window.)*

(READY LIGHTS.)

BHAER. T'ank you, sir. It will gif me pleasure
to come.
   BROOKE. *(Calling from study)* Laurie, come
here a minute, will you?

(Excusing himself, LAURIE *exits to study* R.I.E.*)*

MARCH. *(Placing chair* R. *of table* C.*)* Won't
you sit down?
   MRS. MARCH. *(Going to sofa at fireplace and
picking up rattle and arranging sofa)* No—here,
Professor.

*(*BHAER *sits on sofa and* MRS. MARCH *on stool at
lower end of fireplace.)*

MARCH. My daughter is much interested in
your German translations of Shakespeare, sir.

*(Sitting in chair R. of C. table, which he placed up
stage a bit—Jo sits L. of table C.)*

BHAER. Is it so? Mees Marsche, she say often
she wish a library. I tell her to read him well and
he will help her much; for the study of character
will aid her to read it in the world and paint it with
her pen. I want my people to know him as I know
him, so—*(Hesitates, then in German)*—Ich Ver-
suchte. I make try to put him into the German
tongue.

MARCH. *(Much interested)* It's like trying to
put Schiller into English, I fancy, and quite as dif-
ficult.

BHAER. *(Hesitates, trying to think of English)*
Herr Marsche, that reminds me, Mees Marsche, she
tell me how you luf my Schiller, and so—ich war
so frei—so I make so bold as to bring my copy for
you to see. *(Takes book from pocket; done up in
one of the old-fashioned, luridly illustrated papers
—"The Spread Eagle," or "Fireside Companion,"
in black and white, not comic supplement, as they
were not in existence at the time. At sight of the
paper, BHAER strips it from the book, frowning)*
Ach, one of those sensation papers with their horrid
pictures. I am short-sighted, sir. I did not see
him. The *Spread Eagle*, a family story paper.
These papers are not for young people to read. I
haf no patience with those who make this harm.

MARCH. You are right to put the paper from
you. Young people should not see such things.

(Looks at JO, quietly enjoying her discomfiture.)

BHAER. I would more rather gif a child of mine
gunpowder to play with than this bad trash.

JO. All may not be bad, only silly; and if there

is a demand for it, I don't see any harm in supplying it. Many very respectable people make an honest living out of what are called sensational stories.

(MARCH catches Jo's eye, smiles—she turns away.)

BHAER. *(Vehemently)* There is a demand for whiskey, but I think you and I do not care to sell it. If the respectable people knew what harm they did, they would not think their living honest. They haf no right to put poison in the sugar plum and let the small ones eat it. And the people who write these stories are not only men, but women I grief to say, for in so doing they desecrate their most womanliest nature. For to lif with thieves, murderers and criminals, even dough it is only in imagination, it is to lif in bad company.

(Tearing up the paper—throws it into fireplace, taking care to throw it over grate onto floor behind. Electrician lights small piece of paper in grate. MARCH looking on, evidently amused at the way Jo has taken her lesson. Jo looks uncomfortable. MRS. MARCH, bending over her work, is smiling.)

And I should like to send all the rest after him. *(Rams the last vestige of the paper into grate with poker)* My apologies to you and—*(with a little whimsical smile)*—to Schiller! *(Looking at them all—going R.C.)*

MARCH. *(Rising and meeting BHAER R.C.)* I shall enjoy your Schiller, sir, very much—thank you.

MRS. MARCH. Professor, will you not stay to tea and meet the rest of the family? We should so like to have you.

BHAER. Ach, I am sorrowful I must say no.

(Mrs. March rises) And take myself quickly away from this so pleasant home, but after I tell Mees Marsche that I do myself the pleasure to call this evening, a message for me come that I must heed.

(Jo rises.)

Mrs. March. I am sorry, perhaps another time you will stay.

Bhaer. *(Taking her hand as he speaks)* I shall so gladly come again if you gif me leaf, dear Madame.

Mrs. March. *(Cordially)* We shall always be glad to see you, Professor Bhaer. Good night.

Bhaer. Good night, Madame—good night, sir. —*(Turning to March, then goes to c. in front of table c., turns to them again and says)*—Good night, good night, my friend. *(Very impressive in his manner to Jo.)*

Jo. Good night, Professor Bhaer. *(She picks up his hat, as he starts to go, forgetting it)* Professor Bhaer—— *(She goes with him to door)* Good night, sir.

(Gives Bhaer his hat. As Jo hands hat to Bhaer, he, being nearsighted, looks closely to see what it is—puts hand to head, etc., then with a smile, says quickly)

Bhaer. Good night. *(Exits)*

(Jo stands with back to door, embarrassed, looking at father and mother. Mr. and Mrs. March have exchanged meaning glances.)

March. I suspect that is a wise man.

Mrs. March. And I think he is a good one. *(Starting toward dining room)*

Jo. I knew you would like him.

(Going R. *at back of chair* R. *of table* C., *and pushes chair downstage for father.* MARCH *sits in chair* R. *of table* C., *takes out spectacles, preparing to read Schiller.)*

MRS. MARCH. I must see Hannah about tea, and Father—— *(Gets* MARCH *his hat from dining room then comes downstage)* Do you remember you promised to call on Aunt March to-day?

MARCH. *(A little disappointed)* Oh, yes, I'll go directly, Mother.

(Puts book on table and exits to hall L.I.E. *Exit* MRS. MARCH *to dining room.)*

Jo. *(Speaking to herself—picks up the Schiller)* How nice—Mr. Bhaer looked—so trim and neat—dear old fellow, he couldn't have gotten himself up with more care if he'd been going a-wooing.

(Sits at R. *of table* C., *seems confused at her own suggestion—puts book down as* LAURIE *enters from study, closing door behind him.)*

LAURIE. Everybody gone? I'm glad—*(Goes to* Jo—*tenderly)* for I want to say something I've wanted to say for a long time.

Jo. *(Putting out her hands imploringly)* No, Teddy; please don't. *(*R. *of table* C.)*

LAURIE. *(Determined)* It's no use, Jo; we've got to have it out, and the sooner the better for both of us.

Jo. *(Sighing)* Say what you like, then—I'll listen.

LAURIE. I've loved you ever since I've known you, Jo; couldn't help it. You've been so good to me. I've tried to show it, but you wouldn't let me.

Now I'm going to make you hear, and give me your answer, for I can't go on like this any longer.

Jo. I wanted to save you this. I thought you'd understand——

Laurie. I know you did, but girls are so queer you never know what they mean. They say no when they mean yes, and drive a man out of his wits just for the fun of it.

Jo. I don't. I never wanted you to care for me, so, and I've tried to keep you from it.

Laurie. I thought so, but it was no use. I only loved you all the more—and I've waited and never complained, for I hoped you'd love me, although I'm not half good enough—— *(His voice breaks as he leaves the sentence unfinished)*

Jo. *(Tenderly)* Yes, you are—you're—you're a great deal too good for me, and I'm so proud and fond of you, I don't see why I can't love you as you want me to. I've tried, but I can't change the feeling, and it would be a lie to say I do when I don't.

Laurie. *(Grasping both her hands over R. arm of chair)* Really truly, Jo?

Jo. *(Regretfully)* Really truly, dear. *(Laurie drops her hands, turns away and hides his face on the mantel-shelf, resting it on his arm. Jo goes over remorsefully and pats him on the shoulder)* Oh, Teddy, I'm so sorry! I'm so desperately sorry, I could kill myself, if it would do any good. I wish you wouldn't take it so hard. I can't help it. You know it's impossible for people to make themselves love other people if they don't.

Laurie. *(His face still hidden, voice muffled)* They do sometimes.

Jo. *(Backing away from Laurie)* I don't believe it's the right sort of love, and I'd rather not try it. *(A pause—while Jo stands at C. table—Laurie does not raise his head)* Laurie, I want to tell you something.

LAURIE. *(Starting up quickly, and speaking harshly)* Don't tell me that, Jo; I can't bear it now.

Jo. *(Surprised)* Tell you what?

LAURIE. *(Fiercely)* That you love that old man.

Jo. What old man?

LAURIE. *(R.C.)* That devilish old professor you are always writing and talking about. If you say you love him—— *(Clenching his hands)*

Jo. *(In front of table c.)* Teddy Laurence, I never thought of such a thing! He's good and kind, and the best friend I've got—*(LAURIE makes exclamation)* next to you. He isn't old or—or—devilish —and I know I shall get angry if you abuse my professor.

LAURIE. There—I told you!

Jo. I haven't the least idea of falling in love with him—or anybody else.

LAURIE. But you will after a while, and then what will become of me? *(Turns front)*

Jo. You'll love someone else, too, and forget all this trouble.

LAURIE. *(Stamping his foot to emphasize his words)* I can't love anyone else, and I'll never forget you, Jo—never!

Jo. Teddy, do be reasonable, and take a sensible view of the case.

LAURIE. I won't be reasonable—— *(Turns R. a bit)* I don't want to take what you call a sensible view, it won't help me and it only makes you harder. I don't believe you've got any heart.

Jo. *(Turning, her voice quivering)* I wish I hadn't——

LAURIE. *(Seeing his advantage, putting his arm around her and saying in his most wheedlesome tone)*

Don't disappoint us, dear; everyone expects it. Grandpa has set his heart upon it; your people like it, and I can't get on without you. Say you will and let's be happy. Ah—do—do!

Jo. *(In front of* c. *table, shaking her head sadly)* I can't say yes, truly, so I won't say it at all. *(LAURIE moves away* R.*)* You'll see that I'm right by-and-by and thank me for it.

LAURIE. *(Indignantly)* I'll be hanged if I do.

Jo. Yes, you will. You'll get over this after a while and find some nice, accomplished girl, who will adore you and make a fine mistress of your fine house—— *(Movement of dissent from* LAURIE*)* I shouldn't. I'm homely and awkward and odd and old, and you'd be ashamed of me. And I shouldn't like elegant society, and you would, and you'd hate my scribbling, and I couldn't get on without it, and we should be unhappy and—and—wish we hadn't done it.

LAURIE. Anything more?

Jo. No—nothing more, except that I don't believe I shall ever marry. I love my liberty too well to be in a hurry to give it up for any mortal man.

LAURIE. *(Turning to go)* You'll be sorry some day, Jo. *(Rushes across to* L.I.*)*

Jo. *(Frightened)* Oh, where are you going?

LAURIE. *(To the door by this time)* To the devil!

(WARN CURTAIN.)

(Jo follows LAURIE *to about* L.C. MRS. MARCH, *who has entered quietly by dining-room door, speaking as she comes.)*

MRS. MARCH. *(To* LAURIE, *who is at door)* Laurie, will you ask your grandfather—— *(Jo turns and crosses at back to dining room.* MRS. MARCH *grasps the situation. Going to* LAURIE *at door* L.I., *then seeing that* Jo *has gone, puts a motherly, sympathetic hand on his arm)* My dear, dear boy. I know. Be patient. Jo is right. It is better this way, I am sure.

LAURIE. *(Heartbroken)* I don't want the beautiful, accomplished girl she talks about. I want Jo.

MRS. MARCH. I know, dear, but the hurt will heal, and some time you will find just the right——

AMY. *(Calling from stairway, her voice floating down before she appears)* Laurie, are you there yet? *(*MRS. MARCH *crosses* R.*)*

(She comes down stairway, clad all in white, a ball gown, decollete; shoulders framed in rosebuds and bunches of the buds on her gown; one arm gloved; a pale blue scarf thrown over her golden head, carries old-fashioned bouquet in white paper holder.)

LAURIE. *(Pulling himself together, quickly)* Yes, I was just going.

AMY. *(Down to* LAURIE L., *holds out one arm for him to button glove)* Please! *(Bus.—*LAURIE *bends to fasten her glove,* MRS. MARCH *smiling, looking on)* Thank you. Wilt see me to my coach, Sir Knight? *(*LAURIE *smiles, takes her hand and passes her in front of him so that they are in the doorway)* Good night, Marmee.

MRS. MARCH. *(Tenderly)* Good night, children.

LAURIE. *(Squaring his shoulders and offering* AMY *his arm)* Good night, Mother, I'll look after Amy. *(They exit together,* AMY *first.* Jo, *who has been standing in the dining-room door watching this little scene, not seen by the others, watches them go.* MRS. MARCH, *as if well pleased with the turn of events, exits* R.I.E. *to study.* Jo *comes forward; stands back of table* C. *looking at the door through which* LAURIE *and* AMY *passed.   There is the sound of laughter.* LAURIE *speaks off)* No, Amy, I won't be late.

*(*Jo's *hand falls on* BHAER'S *Schiller lying on the table.   She takes it up, looks at it tenderly and holds it against her breast.)*

MUSIC: *Curtain down.   Rubinstein Song: "Du Bist Wie Eine Blume."*
TIME OF SCENE: *22 minutes.*

MEDIUM CURTAIN

ACT THREE

TIME: *Two and a half years later. Afternoon.*
LIGHTS: *Less than Act I and II. Medium curtain.*
DISCOVERED: HANNAH, *sweeping and putting the rooms to rights, working, sweeping, etc., at doorway* L.; *shakes mat in entry way; puts broom, dustpan, and cloth in entry way, goes to the foot of stairs, listens and smiles mysteriously when* AMY *enters from the study.*
FOR RISE: *Music. Settee is off. Wing chair is back at fireplace. Big, old-fashioned hair-cloth sofa in window center, with crotcheted afghan on it.*
*Baby spot—*R.I.
Amber Bunch L.I.

AMY. *(Enter* R.I., *going to* HANNAH *at stairway)* Hannah! Beth is asleep and I can't wait any longer to see Meg. Is mother upstairs?

HANNAH. *(Chuckling)* Ah, sure they're all upstairs. A warshipin' at the cradle and Miss Meg as happy as a queen.

AMY. Oh, Hannah, isn't it beautiful? What do you suppose Laurie will say when he comes home?

HANNAH. Sure it's a mercy Misther Laurie wazzant here when it happened. We didn't want no hurrycanes around. I must go see about my dinner. *(Starts towards dining-room door)*

AMY. *(At table, up near window)* Have everything very nice, Hannah.

HANNAH. Oh, yis. But me mind is that flustered with Miss Meg it'll be a merrycle if I don't roast the pudding and stuff the turkey with raisins, let alone a boilin' of him in a cloth. *(Exit R.3E.)*

AMY. *(Leaning against the banister L. Looking expectantly upstairs, with a smile)* Think of Meg as a mother—and Marmee a grandmother! *(Smiling proudly)* And I'm an aunt—Aunt Amy! *(Turning and walking proudly downstage L.C.— MRS. MARCH enters softly downstairs)* Oh, Marmee! *(Laughing and making profound bow)* I beg your pardon, Grandma March. *(Backing downstage in front of stairway toward desk L.)*

MRS. MARCH. *(Smiling, goes R.)* John was the first to call me that. It doesn't seem but yesterday since Meg was married.

AMY. Yet, it's more than two years. Oh, Marmee, mayn't I go up now?

MRS. MARCH. Yes, dear. *(AMY starts up with a rush, stops R.C.)* But gently—— *(AMY tiptoes the rest of the way and exits)* Remember the little mother is resting in the next room. MRS. MARCH *crosses and looks into study anxiously, smiles, closes door and turns as MR. LAURENCE enters L.I.E.)*

MR. LAURENCE. *(Comes C., hat in hand, smiling)* Good morning, Madame; this is a happy household to-day.

MRS. MARCH. Yes; we are very happy and very thankful.

MR. LAURENCE. John was over early to tell us the good news.

MRS. MARCH. It was an anxious night, but joy came with the morning.

MR. LAURENCE. Is Jo going with me to the station to meet my boy Laurie?

MRS. MARCH. She isn't back from Aunt March's yet, but if she is too late, please remember she's asked to be the first to tell Laurie about Meg, so don't even hint.

Mr. Laurence. Not a hint, ma'am. But it can't be a complete surprise, you know. How is Beth?

Mrs. March. She is asleep in the study.

Mr. March. *(Enters down the stairs, very proud, comedy strut, coming down* l.c.*)* Good morning.

Mr. Laurence. Good morning, sir—— *(Shaking hands)* This should be the proudest day of your life——

Mr. March. *(Smiling)* I think it is.

Mr. Laurence. *(Going to* l.i.*)* Laurie and I should be back in half an hour. Tell Miss Jo I promise secrecy.

(Exit l.i.e. Mr. March, *closes door after him; turns and looks upstairs where* Meg *and babies are.* Mrs. March *does same. Then* Mr. March *holds out his arms to* Mrs. March *and she comes into them—embrace and kiss.)*

Mr. March. Mother!

Mrs. March. Father!

Mr. March. Meg and John are like two children with a new toy; and Amy, bless her, hovers over the cradle like a golden-haired Madonna.

Mrs. March. *(Going to front of stairway)* She will get her model from life now, dear little girl. I presume she has started a sketch already.

Mr. March. Well, when I came down it wasn't art, but finery. *(Starts to go* r.*)* She and Meg were discussing some problem about ribbons and poor John seemed helpless.

(Going r. *to mantel.)*

Mrs. March. Imagine poor John knowing anything about ribbons.

*(Starts up staircase, Mr. March at mantel, takes
up letters and wrapped book, etc.)*

Jo. *(Enters L.I.E., breathless—taking off things)*
I ran all the way from Aunt March's. She's as
proud as a peacock and tries not to show it, snort-
ing and scolding one minute and asking questions the
next. I know I am too late to meet Teddy!

Mrs. March. Yes; Mr. Laurence left here a
few minutes ago.

*(Exits upstairs and Jo takes off her things during
the preceding speeches and puts them on small
seat under stairway—sits L. of table C.)*

Mr. March. *(Going to R. of table C.)* Jo, this
looks like a book for you! *(Hands her package—
then sits R. of table C., takes out spectacles, preparing to read letters)*

Jo. For me? *(Undoing parcel)* Father—it's
Professor Bhaer's English translation of Schiller—
author's copy—autographed—and with an inscrip-
tion in his own hand-writing. *(Looking conscious
as she studies it closely)*

March. Oh, what has he written?

Jo. Why, Father, the dear old fellow has ac-
tually credited me with being his inspiration.

*(Amy enters on stairs, almost running, so eager to
start her Madonna. Jo and Mr. March laugh
quietly. Amy goes to sofa in window C. and begins sketching.)*

Mr. March. Perhaps you were his inspiration,
Jo.

Jo. Much more likely that he's been mine, for
he's made me ashamed of writing trash.

Mr. March. I wish that philosophy paid better

in this money-loving world and then my girl wouldn't have to be writing lurid tales.

Jo. Well, Plato—— *(*MARCH *smiles)* "The Duke's Daughter" paid the butcher's bill; "A Phantom Hand," put down a new carpet; and "The Curse of the Conventrys" proved the blessing of the Marches in the way of groceries and gowns; so the inside of my head can at least take care of the outside.

MR. MARCH. How is the book coming on? Any news from the publisher?

Jo. Well, they sent back the first chapters; thought they were dull.

MR. MARCH. Oh!

Jo. So did I, but I've started 'em out again, and now—*(Laughs)*—I'm sitting like Patience on a hard chair smiling at an inkstand.

MR. MARCH. Life is your college, dear, and you will graduate with honors, I know.

Jo. Well, disappointment must be good for me, I get so much of it, and the constant thumping Fate gives me may prove a mellowing process, so I shall be a ripe and sweet old pippin before I die.

MR. MARCH. *(Rises. laughs heartily, going R.)* All the philosophy in the house is not in the study, I see.

(Exits to study R.I.)

AMY. *(Coming down to back of c. table, back to table, holding out the sketch)* Look, Jo, see my modern Madonna.

Jo. It's great, Amy, you have Meg's expression exactly. You're going to be the real genius of the March family, after all. I'm the grub and you're the butterfly.

AMY. Jo! How can you say that? Think of all you've done for all of us. Why, it's you who have made me ambitious to do my share. How I shall work when I get to Rome. Think of it, Jo— I sail in less than a month! Wasn't it good of Aunt Curtis to invite me?

Jo. Splendid, little Raphael, splendid!

Amy. Do you think I'm selfish to go, Jo? Father and mother both tell me to, but with Beth so ill it seems as if I were leaving such a burden for you to carry alone.

Jo. Oh, don't think about me. Take your chance and make all you can of it. Laurie and his Grandpa will be going over soon and they'll see that you have a perfectly plummy time.

Mrs. March. *(Comes down the stairs—goes to window* l.*)* Here comes Laurie, girls!

(Jo rises, stands in front of table c. Amy *puts her drawing board at* l. *foot of sofa and drops down* r.*)*

Laurie. *(Enters* l.i.e.*—goes to* Mrs. March's *arms)* How do you do, everybody! College is great, but oh, I say—it's good to be home! *(Takes both* Mrs. March's *hands, looks into her eyes, smiling)* Yes, Mother, it's all right! *(Kisses her)*

Jo. *(Rapturously)* My Teddy—oh, my Teddy!

Laurie. *(Throws hat on table* c.; *goes to* Jo, c. *—tenderly)* Dear Jo, are you glad to see me?

Jo. Glad? My blessed boy, words can't express my gladness.

Laurie. *(Goes to* Amy r.c., *as if to embrace her—*Amy *starts back, a little embarrassed)* Amy— *(Pause)*—you're a picture in that gown!

Amy. I'm glad you like the frock, Laurie—I made it myself.

(Study door opens and Beth, *carrying a Paisley shawl on* l. *arm, enters with* Mr. March. Amy

and Jo *go up to window* c., *also* MRS. MARCH.
They fix the sofa and cushions for BETH.)

MR. MARCH.   My boy!

BETH.   Laurie!

LAURIE.   (*Crossing to* BETH, *kissing her*)   Beth! How is our little Tranquillity? Have you been gaining since I went away? (*Realizes the change in her*)

BETH.   (*Smiling*)   Yes, Laurie, I am better, I hope.

LAURIE.   May I escort you to your throne, Queen Bess? I'm sorry I'm minus my velvet cloak. (*Bows in courteous manner*—BETH *smiles at him*)

Jo.   Here, Teddy! (*Fixing the pillows of sofa in window* R.C.)   Over here in the sunshine. (*Goes* L.)

(*Bus. of settling* BETH. MR. MARCH *and* LAURIE *help* BETH *to sofa*—MARCH *spreads the shawl over her;* AMY *spreads a little white shawl over* BETH'S *shoulders.* HANNAH *enters.*)

LAURIE.   (*Dropping downstage a little above* c. *table to the* R.)   Bless my soul, I forgot not to make a racket, and here's Hannah poking her head in the door to warn me: "Shake not thy gory locks at me——!" Hannah, come hither!

(HANNAH *approaches* R., *carrying turkey in right hand.* LAURIE *embraces her heartily*—HANNAH *looks at him adoringly.*)

HANNAH.   (*Laughs*)   Oh, Misther Laurie, you're the Blarney, but you're bonnier than ever, and that's the truth.

(*Suddenly becomes aware of the turkey she is car-*

rying, covers it up with apron and retires up-stage R. *a bit.* MARCH *goes down to fireplace as* HANNAH *goes up* R.)

LAURIE. *(Covering his face with his hands as if to hide his blushes)* Oh, don't, Hannah! Where is Brooke? And how's the little Mamma? Why didn't you tell me before I got home? Grandpa is so mysterious, he refuses to say whether it's a boy or a girl.

HANNAH. *(Grinning—coming forward)* Miss Jo sez——

JO. *(Goes to staircase)* Never mind what Miss Jo says. Wait, Teddy, not a word from anyone—mind!

(Exits upstairs with a rush, HANNAH *retires up-stage* R. *behind armchair at fireplace.)*

LAURIE. *(Dropping down* R. *to* MARCH) Jupiter Ammon! What does she mean?

MR. MARCH. You wait, Laurie.

*(*BROOKE *appears on the stairs, comes to* L.C.)*

LAURIE. Ah! Greetings, Father Brooke—— *(Going* L.C. *to* BROOKE) How is Mrs. Brooke and the little Brooke?

BROOKE. *(Shaking hands)* All doing nicely, thank you.

(Enter JO *at top of stairs with large bundle on a pillow covered with blanket.* BROOKE *retires* L., JO *comes down* L.C. *to* LAURIE.)

JO. *(Calls)* Shut your eyes! *(She advances with measured stride.* LAURIE *backs to the* R. *corner behind,* BROOKE *follows)* Shut your eyes and hold out your arms. *(Backing* LAURIE *across stage to* R.)

LAURIE. *(At study door* R.I.*)* No, thank you!
I'd rather not. I shall drop or smash it as sure as
Fate!

JO. Then you sha'n't see your nevvy!

LAURIE. *(Holding out his arms)* I will—I will
—only you must be responsible for damages.

JO. Shut your eyes! *(LAURIE closes his eyes—
JO puts bundle into his arms. The others, dropping
down to R.C. above JO and LAURIE, looking on. JO
puts back the blanket, uncovering the little heads of
the twins)* Now look!

*(LAURIE opens his eyes, looks at babies, face changes
from curiosity to bewilderment. JO so overcome she sits on the floor and holds her sides.
R.C.)*

LAURIE. Twins, by Jupiter! Take 'em quick—
somebody—I'm going to laugh, and I shall drop
'em!

*(Goes into roar of laughter. MRS. MARCH and
AMY go up to BETH. BROOKE rescues the
babies, stops up L.C. Holding babies so their
heads are toward audience. After laugh,
BROOKE goes up to group around BETH. HAN-
NAH exits, laughing, R.3E. MARCH goes with
BROOKE.)*

JO. Well, I set my heart on surprising you, and
I flatter myself, I've done it.

LAURIE. *(Wiping his eyes)* Was never more
staggered in my life. *(Goes to L. of JO)* Isn't it
fun? Are they boys? Let's have another look.
What are you going to call them? *(AMY drops
down to R.—BROOKE drops down to L. of LAU-
RIE)* Here, Jo—— *(JO slowly rises)* When you

get through unfolding like an animated puzzle, hold me up, will you? For, upon my word, it's one too many for me! *(LAURIE drops into Jo's arms, goes to her L.)*

BROOKE. *(L.C., proudly to LAURIE and Jo)* Boy and girl—aren't they beauties?

LAURIE. Most remarkable children I ever saw. Which is which? *(Bus.—BROOKE can't tell—LAURIE laughs)*

Jo. Amy put a blue ribbon on the boy and a pink on the girl, French fashion, so you can always tell. Besides, one has blue eyes and one brown. Kiss them, Uncle Teddy.

LAURIE. *(Hesitating)* I'm afraid they mightn't like it.

Jo. *(Teasing)* Of course they will. Do it this minute, sir.

(LAURIE screws up his face, takes one peek at the bundle, then another. Squall from the bundle and everyone laughs.)

LAURIE. There! I knew they wouldn't like it. *(Baby cry)* That's the boy—look at him kick—he hits out like a good one. Now then, young Brooke, pitch into a man of your own size, will you? *(BROOKE swings the babies toward LAURIE)*

AMY. *(Proudly)* He's to be named John Laurence, and the girl Margaret after mother and grandmother. We shall call her Daisy, so as not to have two Megs in the family, and as we can't have two Johns either, I suppose the "mannie" will be Jack unless we find a better name.

LAURIE. *(Hand on BROOKE's shoulder, seriously)* John and little John. *(Teasingly)* Why—name him Demijohn! *(BROOKE glares at him)* And call him Demi for short.

(BROOKE *turns away with mock indignation, going to stair.*)

Jo. (*Clapping her hands*) Daisy and Demi! Just the thing! I knew Teddy would do it.

(BROOKE *exits upstairs with babies*—ALL *laugh.*)

MR. MARCH. (*Laughing, goes to door* L.I. *as* BROOKE *goes to stairway*) All this, while very pleasant, isn't preparing next Sunday's talk. I'll seek inspiration under the trees. (*Exits* L.I.E.*)*
AMY. My drawing lesson's at four—it's time I started. (*Going to* L.C.*)*
LAURIE. I'll walk with you, Mademoiselle, if I may.
AMY. Avec plaisir, monsieur. (*Goes to closet to get hat*)
MRS. MARCH. And I must help Hannah. Jo, will you look after Beth?
Jo. (*Goes* L. *to desk to get her writing box*) Yes, Marmee, I'm going to write and cuddle Bethy as soon as the excitement is over.

(MRS. MARCH *exits* R.U.E.*)*

BETH. (*Having picked up* AMY'S *drawing board*) Oh, Amy, how lovely—how lovely!
AMY. (*Goes to* BETH *at window* C.) Beth, I didn't want you to see it until it was finished—I was doing it for you.
BETH. How good everyone is to me. You always make me think of beauty, Amy, and of the gladness of the spring. You are our March sunshine, dear.

(*Reaching up her arm and pulling* AMY *down to kiss her;* AMY *fixes the pillows and makes her*

comfy during the following scene. Jo *goes to*
L. *of table* C.)

LAURIE. Won't you come, Jo? *(Goes to her)*
Come, don't be thorny, a fellow deserves a little
petting after a long grind in college.

Jo. Amy will pet you. I'm busy.

LAURIE. Amy isn't given to petting. *(Puts
hands on her shoulders and says in wheedling tone:)*
Do you hate your boy and want him to go away?

Jo. *(Petting his face in sisterly, fond fashion)*
You know I don't, Teddy dear, but Beth needs me
now. *(Her voice breaks)*

LAURIE. *(Bending until his face rests on her
hair)* I understand, Jo. *(Voices outside)*

MR. MARCH. *(Outside)* Come right in—they'll
all be glad to see you.

BHAER. And I to see them—I have waited long
to greet them all again.

(Enter, followed by MARCH—BHAER *carries forget-
me-nots in his hand—stops as he sees* LAURIE
with his arm around Jo—LAURIE *starts back—*
Jo *embarrassed.)*

Jo. Oh, Mr. Bhaer! *(Goes to him—then stops
and turns abruptly away; twitches collar, smoothes
hair, frenzied attempt to make herself tidy)* Oh, I
look such a fright! *(Turns again to* BHAER, *holding out hand)* When did you come? You remember Laurie, don't you?

*(*BHAER *starts to hand her flowers, gets embarrassed, changes flowers to other hand, shakes
hands with* Jo.)

BHAER. *(Ready Robin at window)* Indeed I
do, most pleasantly. *(Crosses to him)*

LAURIE. How do you do, Professor Bhaer?

BHAER. Very well, I tank you. *(Turning to* Jo, *who drops down* L, *half hands her the flowers, then takes them back again)* I arrif only this morning, Mees Marche. How is the leetle sick one?

MR. MARCH. Come right up here and speak to her, Professor.

BHAER. *(Places hat on table* C. *as he goes up with* MR. MARCH—*crossing to* BETH, *and handing her the flowers)* May I venture to offer these flowers to my leetle friend? They make me think of your eyes.

*(*MARCH *goes to* L. *end of sofa,* BHAER *at* R. *end.)*

BETH. Oh, thank you, sir.

*(*BETH *takes the flowers.* Jo *gets* BHAER'S *book from* C. *table and stands with* LAURIE *by desk* —LAURIE *upstage facing front,* Jo *with back to audience.)*

AMY. Mr. Bhaer, it is good to see you here again.

BHAER. And it is goot to be here, Mees Amy. *(*AMY *goes into dining room for vase. He turns and sees* Jo *and* LAURIE *together; comes down* C. *to* R. *of* C. *table.* MARCH *is back of* C. *table)* And may I congratulate this happy household? *(Pause—looks between* Jo *and* LAURIE— *they separate,* MARCH *takes in the situation)* Motherhood is the deepest and tenderest experience in a woman's life.

Jo. And may I congratulate you, sir, on the beautiful book? *(*BHAER *goes to* Jo, L.*)* I never had anything dedicated to me before—and to begin with Schiller!

(Puts the book on desk. As LAURIE *and* MARCH
go to BETH, AMY *returning at once, puts* BETH'S
*flowers in vase and places them on window sill
and sits* R. *on sofa.* LAURIE *sits in chair at* R.,
head of sofa and MARCH *sits on small stool at
foot of sofa* L. AMY *sits on sofa beside* BETH
*—threads her needle for her—*BETH *is sewing
on the little baby jacket.)*

BHAER. As your goot Fadder says, Mees
Marche, always begin with the best. But you—you
have been ill, my friend? *(Looking at her closely)*

JO. Not ill, but a little tired, and worried about
Beth.

BHAER. Ah, yes, I know, for the goot Fadder
he has told me, and my heart, he grieves for you.
I wish I could help—do something.

JO. Thank you, sir, but nothing can help me just
now—except to have Beth get well—— *(Places
her hand on* BHAER'S *arm—her voice breaking)* She
seems to be slipping away from us.

BHAER. *(Takes* JO's *hand)* Dot is in Gott's
hands, Mees Marche; but the spring comes.—*(*LAU-
RIE *rises and arranges* BETH'S *pillows—*BHAER
turns and sees this)—And dot should help my little
friend. *(Gets hat from table* C.*)* I know you may
tink of me—he is a stupid old fellow; he will not
see. But I haf an eye, and I see much; I haf a
heart, and I feel—I tink it besser to say not what I
feel—now. *(Starts to go* L.I.E.*)*

JO. *(Quickly—putting out her hand)* Oh, you
are not going so soon? *(*BHAER *turns)* Mother will
be in directly.

                    (READY LIGHTS.)

BHAER. Tank you, but I must go. *(Takes* JO's
hand, looks across at LAURIE*)* I tink it is time.
(Almost as if he were putting her out of his life

forever) May the happiness which you haf so richly deserved be yours for always, my friend. Good-bye. *(Opens door)*

Jo. *(Surprised)* Good-bye?

BHAER. *(Turns, with sad little smile)* Well, den, let us say Auf Wiedersehn. *(Exits L.I.E.)*

(Jo stands at window L., looking after him. ROBIN chirps.)

BETH. Listen—that's my robin! *(LAURIE rises)* See how he struts and tries to show off. He's singing for his supper. Amy, will you bring me some crumbs?

(MR. MARCH turns, looks L. ROBIN stops.)

Jo. *(Starts quietly for dining room)* I'll get them, dear.

MR. MARCH. Why, where's the professor?

Jo. *(Without turning)* He's gone. *(Exit R.3E. LAURIE looks after her)*

AMY. We must hurry, I'll be late for my lesson.

(Picks up drawing-board, kisses BETH and goes down to door L.; then LAURIE starts L., turns back, as if he divined a change in BETH—and kisses her.)

LAURIE. Good-bye for a little while, Beth. You must hurry and get well.

BETH. Yes, yes—I shall be well soon, Laurie. *(LAURIE goes down to back of C. table, stops, realizing BETH's condition. AMY almost says in pantomime "Are you coming?"—They exit together L.I.E. MR. MARCH is standing looking out of window— when BETH speaks he goes and sits beside her on sofa. BETH holds up a little baby jacket)* See,

Father, I wanted to finish it before the babies came. Will you take it to Meg, please, and tell her that every stitch means love for her?

MR. MARCH. Yes, dear, I will.

(Takes jacket, rises, faces front, holding out jacket, looks at it, then at BETH, who has lain back on pillows, then exits upstairs.)

Jo. *(Enters with dish of crumbs, opens window)* Here we are, dear.

(Sits back of BETH, holding her up. After BETH throws out crumbs, ROBIN chirps again.)

BETH. See, Jo, how tame he is. Dear little fellow. I hope *he* comes back next spring. *(BETH shivers and lies back)*

Jo. Oh, you're cold, dearie. *(Closes windows)* Aren't you tired of sitting on the sofa, and sha'n't I tuck you up in the big chair by the fire?

BETH. Yes, please, and—— *(Handing over the work basket)* Please put these things away. The needle is so heavy—and I am tired——

Jo. *(Turns armchair, throws pillows onto floor R.C., up to sofa, very gently lifts BETH—says:)* Upsy daisy! *(Places BETH in chair, then pushes chair downstage to about R.C. a little R. in front of fireplace)* Now I'll give you a nice long ride. *(Puts pillows under feet and shawl over her legs. Lights change to light amber, dim foots and 1st border accordingly)* Are you all right now, little sister?

(BETH'S lines must be spoken sweetly and happily— without tears or fear of death; trying to make it easy for others. Simplicity and faith the keynote.)

BETH. Yes, thank you. *(Jo sits on floor at L. of chair—a little pause)* Jo, I thought of Meg all night long, as I lay awake. Dear, happy little mother in that room upstairs. I thought of the angel sent to show those little babies the way to this life and—— *(Reaching for Jo's hand)* Jo—perhaps waiting to show some weary soul the way to—a more perfect life—how strange the coming and the going—and how beautiful—I think I've just been waiting to see Meg's babies. *(Jo looks quickly at her sister and shows that she understands at last the nearness of the parting. BETH smiles tenderly. Jo hides her face in BETH's lap. BETH smoothes her hair. Jo sobs)* Jo, dear, I'm glad you understand. I've wanted to tell you, but I couldn't. Will you tell the others for me?

Jo. *(Quietly sobbing)* Beth! What are you saying? You're not going—— God wouldn't be so cruel.

BETH. *(Holding her close, for a moment the stronger of the two)* Hush, Jo! This morning—I watched the sunrise. As the darkness faded into the gray and violet . . . I watched and waited. The sky got rosy and beautiful—, and then it seemed as if everything stood still—as if God's hand had rested on the earth for a moment—and then—the glory of the sun! It seemed like going through a long, dark passage—or a grave—and suddenly coming in to light, and, Jo, dear, I felt for the first time—*the nearness* of God. I knew that the Angel of Life was waiting for me. *(With radiant face)*

Jo. Beth! I'm not going to give you up——

BETH. But I sha'n't be far away. I'll go on helping all I can, dear. The only hard part is leaving you all. I'm not afraid—but it seems as if I should be homesick for you even in Heaven.

MRS. MARCH. *(Enters from dining room, comes R. of chair, speaking as she comes down)* Beth, dear, come with mother—— *(Looks at* BETH *and sees her sinking condition—takes her wrist and* R. *hand to feel pulse, left hand to forehead)* I want you to lie down.

BETH. I think I will, Marmee. *(Jo takes shawl and pillows, remaining on knees.* BETH *rises with rapt expression as if seeing a beautiful vision.* MRS. MARCH *helps* BETH *to door* R.I.*)* Tell them soon, Jo—very soon——

(Jo has risen, takes BETH'S *hand and kisses it. Jo nods, too overcome to speak.)*

MRS. MARCH. Come, dear.

(A light in R.I. *beams on* BETH *just before she exits, as she pauses, in door. Jo closes the door softly behind* BETH*—passes her hand lovingly over* BETH'S *chair, takes up her pillow, kisses it and breaks into sobs, sinks onto sofa, burying face in pillow.* MARCH *and* BROOKE *laugh outside.)*

MR. MARCH. *(Laughing, he and* BROOKE *coming downstairs)* Daisy certainly shows a proper appreciation of her new finery. *(As they reach* L.C., BROOKE *filling pipe. Lights change to dark amber. Foots and* 1st *border accordingly)* Oh, John!

BROOKE. *(Laughing)* Can't be a bad example to my son, and I must smoke, Father. Will you join me for a turn in the garden?

MR. MARCH. *(Going to door* L.*)* You shouldn't begin by hiding your vices, John. But I'll go——

(They step into the hallway, where JOHN *stops to light his pipe.* MEG'S *voice upstairs is heard crooning an old lullaby to her babies. "Oh, hush thee, my baby; Thy sire was a knight," etc. This*

*continues intermittently and softly to the end of
the act. Jo goes down and sits* L. *of table* C.
*where her small writing desk is, and tries to
write—looks up—her head in her hands. Study
door opens and* MRS. MARCH *enters—closes
door softly.)*

MRS. MARCH. *(Unemotionally—restrained)* Jo,
dear, go to Beth. She is asking for you.

Jo. Yes, Mother. *(Exits to study)*

*(*MRS. MARCH *starts to the stairs; just as she reaches
foot of stairs,* MR. MARCH *laughs outside.)*

MRS. MARCH. *(Turning)* Father—Father——
(To L. *of* C.*)*

MR. MARCH. *(Enters, followed by* BROOKE*)*
Mother—what is it?

BROOKE. Is Beth worse?

MRS. MARCH. *(Quietly, but tensely)* It's the
end, I'm afraid. She asked for Jo. I must send
Hannah for Amy.

BROOKE. I'll go.

MRS. MARCH. No, you must stay with Meg; she
can't be told yet.

MR. MARCH. *(Going back of* C. *table)* I'll send
Hannah.

(Exits R.3E. MRS. MARCH *crosses in a daze to* C.*)*

BROOKE. *(Putting his arm about her)* It may
not be the end—only another sinking spell, Mother.
Don't give up hope.

MRS. MARCH. Oh, John, I'm afraid—— *(As
she starts for the study door,* MARCH *re-enters)* I'm
afraid—— *(Goes to study, places hand on door
knob—turns, meets* MARCH *in front of closed door.*
MRS. MARCH *breaks down, puts her head against
his shoulder. He holds her close)*

MR. MARCH. There, there—my little Spartan Mother! We're not going to sadden Beth's last moments with our tears.

(MRS. MARCH *pulls herself together, looks up into his face with a brave smile.* MR. MARCH *opens door,* MRS. MARCH *enters slowly, slight pause —then* MR. MARCH *follows.* BROOKE *looks at door, then turns, looks up stairs where* MEG *is singing to the babies. Slight pause—*LAURIE *enters* L.I., *quietly, to* L.C.)

WARN CURTAIN.)

LAURIE. Brooke, what's the matter? I saw Hannah flying down the street. When I spoke to her she burst out crying and hurried on. Is it Beth?

BROOKE. *(Goes* R.*)* Yes.

LAURIE. Is she worse? *(*BROOKE *nods)* Where is Jo?

BROOKE. *(Nodding toward study)* They are all in there with Beth. She must have taken a turn for the worse and—— *(Stops as* LAURIE *looks beyond him. Study door opens and* MARCH *comes out, closes door, crosses to* BROOKE *at* R. *of table* C., *without seeing either of the boys.* BROOKE *puts out his hand to* MARCH'S *shoulder)* Father!

*(*MARCH *looks up for a moment, bows his head and exits to garden, pausing for a second to lift his head to the light—*JOHN *and* LAURIE *look at each other, realizing* BETH'S *death.)*

LAURIE. *(Gently)* Dear little Beth. Does Amy know?

BROOKE. Not yet. They sent Hannah for her.

LAURIE. I'll go and meet her.

BROOKE. *(Starting)* Better wait here, I must go to Meg.

(Up to first landing—pauses a moment as he hears MEG'S *voice, pulls himself together and exits—* MEG'S *singing stops.* LAURIE *walks slowly up to window* R.C., *looks out of it, evidently waiting for* AMY.)

AMY. *(Enters, running, throws her hat on* C. *table—going to* R.C.) Laurie, what is it? Is Beth *very* ill?

LAURIE. *(Coming to* AMY *quickly, taking both her hands and speaking very gently)* No, dear; Beth is WELL at last.

*(*AMY *looks up at him, realizes the truth, goes to* BETH'S *chair, drops to her knees beside it, hides her face in arms on chair, sobbing quietly.)*

AMY. Oh!

LAURIE. *(Goes to her)* Don't, dear, don't— Little Amy, this isn't the *end*—it's the beginning. This is the time for gladness—not for tears! *(Pause with awe and inspiration as they listen. Bird song)* Don't you get her message from the other side?

(This must be spoken with great simplicity and sincerity.)

(The Bird is heard singing just outside the window; the low, sweet, late afternoon song of the sunset hour. At BETH'S *chair,* LAURIE *has one arm across* AMY'S *shoulders, looking at her. Her head is resting against him. He looks at her with growing tenderness.)*

MEDIUM SLOW CURTAIN

(As Bird is heard AMY *looks up. Hold picture for*

2nd curtain. No calls. No music for curtain
down. Overture between Acts III and IV,
"Sunny South Overture.")

(Time of act: 30 minutes.)

ACT FOUR

TIME: *Eighteen months later, October, 1868. A golden October afternoon.*

SCENE: *The Harvest Home. Plumfield. "A mellow October day, when the air was full of an exhilarating freshness, which made the spirits rise and the blood dance healthily in the veins. The old orchard was in holiday attire; goldenrods and asters fringed the mossy walls; grasshoppers skipped briskly in the sere grass, and crickets chirped like fairy pipers at a feast; squirrels were busy with their small harvesting; birds twittered their adieux from the alders on the lawn; and every tree stood ready to send down its shower of red or yellow apples at the first shake. Everybody was there; everybody laughed and sang, climbed up and tumbled down; everybody declared that there had never been such a perfect day, or such a jolly set to enjoy it."*

ACT IV

Orchard drop in perspective. Two cut drops. One platform three feet wide, ten inches high runs back of wall between cut drop to C. Padded step from platform to stage level. Four-foot stone wall and rustic gate from L.1. to L.3. Then across the back—with opening center. Big oak tree with bench R. Six wood wings.

SET FOR ACT IV: *An Autumn orchard, with brook in middle distance, connected with front stage by small rustic bridge. Vistas of red and yellow-leaved trees, with paths between. A clearing in center stage, covered with turf. Garden seat arranged under tree* R. *at edge of clearing, but not to obstruct views up paths leading off between trees, right and left. Stone wall covered with vines—across the back—opening in* C.—*rustic swing gate* L.I.E. *Air filled with Autumn sounds. Practical apple orchard.*

LIGHTS: *Straw throughout act. Medium Curtain.*

MUSIC AT RISE: *Curtain up: "The Birks of Aberfeldy."*

DISCOVERED: *As the curtain rises slowly,* BROOKE *is lying under a tree,* R.C. *at* R., *his hat over his eyes, pipe in his mouth, hands under head, attitude of perfect repose.* MEG *sitting beside him on bench under tree. Get the atmosphere of the Autumn scene for a few moments, song of birds, crickets, ripple from brook; the orchestra playing softly and rather slowly, "The Birks of Aberfeldy."*

MEG. *(Dropping her sewing and looking up at the trees, off* L., *noting the beauty all about her. She evidently sees something that interests her in a nearby tree, for she speaks to her husband in a subdued voice)* John! John! *(*JOHN *sits up, looks* L. MEG *puts her hand on his shoulder)* See that darling little squirrel.

BROOKE. *(Lazily sitting up and following the direction in which her unlifted finger is pointing, taking his pipe from his mouth and emitting a puff of smoke)* That isn't a squirrel, it's a chipmunk. *(He drops back on the ground and continues smoking, another pause)*

MEG. Smarty! It's such a beautiful place. *(Smiling)* Aunt March certainly did the March family one good turn in leaving dear old Plumfield to Jo.

BROOKE. *(Sits up and puts his hand on her knee, teasingly)* She certainly did them another—look at the husband she provided for you.

MEG. *(Cuffing him)* Conceit, well, there's one thing; you're useful as well as ornamental—but what will Jo do with Plumfield?

BROOKE. *(Laughs)* Why, I think her plan is a fine one—to turn it into a home school for boys.

(AMY enters laughing L 1.—JOHN sits up.)

AMY. *(Going to them)* Meg, you should see Father and the babies. He's trying to teach them the alphabet.

BROOKE. The alphabet?

AMY. Yes, with his *legs!*

BROOKE and MEG. *(Exclaim and laugh)* His legs!

AMY. Lying on his back, Demi on the ground beside him, their legs in the air making V's and W's while—*(Showing with her fingers)*—Daisy looks on in wide-eyed wonder.

(MEG and BROOKE roar; AMY drops down to turf beside them.)

MEG. With a philosopher for a grandfather and a tutor for a father, my son will soon be having bumps over his eyes and asking unanswerable questions.

BROOKE. The Plumfield School has certainly started.

AMY. I wish it had. I do want Jo to realize her old dream of plenty of boys and plenty of freedom.

MEG. But it isn't practical, dear. Jo is a born tomboy, I know, but even she can't run a boys' school, without the right teachers and enough money.

BROOKE. *(Insinuatingly)* But fond parents *have* been known to pay.

AMY. Yes, but it would be just like Jo to gather up every little ragged urchin that needed a home. She'd adopt a whole orphan asylum if she could. *(Turns up left)*

BROOKE. Well, then, I don't see anything for it except to have her marry a rich man. *(AMY turns)*

MEG. *(Trying to hush him on AMY's account)* John Brooke, are you turning matchmaker?

BROOKE. No, I leave such trivialities to my wife —but wouldn't it be nice if—Laurie—— *(Gets up on knees. AMY gets up and moves a little away L.U.)*

MEG. John! *(Motions him to be quiet, then putting on a little affair of lace and flowers she is making; breaking in to change subject; trying to cover up JOHN's breaks)* John! How do you like my new millinery?

BROOKE. It's very pretty. Is that what you call a breakfast cap?

MEG. My dear man, it's my very best go-to-the-concert and theatre bonnet.

BROOKE. *(Sitting up and looking interested)* I beg your pardon. *(MEG illustrates the bonnet. BROOKE puts his arms about her)* It's a love of a bonnet, but I prefer the face inside. *(Kisses her)*

(Enter MR. LAURENCE and MRS. MARCH from L.3E. AMY joins them as they come downstage, takes MR. LAURENCE's arm.)

MR. LAURENCE. *(Speaking as they stroll down—* L. *of* C.) This is a fine old place and it's been in your family for generations. I wish Miss Jo would let me help her finance her scheme.

MRS. MARCH. *(*R. *of* C.) I'm afraid her plan isn't feasible. She's no more idea of business than a baby.

AMY. *(*L.*)* That's why she's so dear, Mr. Laurence.

MEG. Oh, why, when Aunt March left Jo the old place, didn't she include money enough to run it?

MRS. MARCH. I'm not sure that I altogether approve of Jo's plan. She's making a name for herself with her writing, and since our little Beth left us, that has been her one pleasure.

*(*LAURIE *enters from* L.3 *to* C.)

MR. LAURENCE. *(Not seeing him)* Where is Jo?

MEG. I think she's somewhere about the place with Laurie.

LAURIE. *(Laughing* C.) Oh, no she isn't. She's showing the professor over Plumfield, and they're building educational castles in the air—a castle on every acre.

*(All laugh—*JOHN *lying down in front of* MEG.)

MRS. MARCH. Yes, and quite forgetting that there are hungry men to feed. I think I'll tell Hannah to have tea out here under the trees.

AMY. Oh, do, Marmee, it will be beautiful.

MEG. *(Shaking* BROOKE*)* Get up, you lazy boy. *(Rises)* And help me collect the babies—— *(They all laugh)* It's their sleepy time, remember.

BROOKE. Behold, a henpecked husband! *(On knees, then rises—they all laugh at him)*

MR. LAURENCE. *(Following* MRS. MARCH *out of gate to* L.) I seek the philosopher of the apple orchard!

(MEG *crosses to gate* L.)

BROOKE.   Aren't you going to wait for me?
MEG.   Come along, slow poke.

(MEG, BROOKE, MRS. MARCH *and* MR. LAURENCE *exit* L., *through gate laughing and talking together.* AMY *starts to follow them, but* LAURIE *intercepts her.)*

LAURIE.   Amy, wait! What a day and what a place! Somehow it makes me think of that old garden at Valrosa. Do you remember?
AMY.   Shall I ever forget? You used to read to me by the hour, while I sketched.
LAURIE.   *(Laughing)* And lectured. Don't forget that, please.
AMY.   *(Contritely)* Did I lecture, Laurie?
LAURIE.   Well, rather—regular rousers, but it did me good, made me ashamed of my lazy ways. *(Going up* C.) When do you begin your great work of art, Raphaella?
AMY.   Never. Rome took all the vanity out of me, for after seeing the wonders there, I felt too insignificant to live, and gave up all my foolish hopes in despair.
LAURIE.   Why should you, with so much energy and talent?
AMY.   That's just why. Because talent isn't genius, and no amount of energy can make it so. I want to be great or nothing. *(Goes* R. *to seat under tree)* I won't be a commonplace dauber, so I don't intend to try any more. *(Sits on* R. *bench)*
LAURIE.   I'm glad of it. *(Going to her)*
AMY.   Why?

LAURIE. Because—because—I—I—well, I don't think a career is suited to you, Amy—you belong——

AMY. Yes——

LAURIE. That is—Amy——

AMY. Yes, Laurie——

LAURIE. I—I——

AMY. Yes, Laurie——

LAURIE. *(To* c., *floundering hopelessly)* I've found those sketches you made of the trail at Vevay.

AMY. *(Rises)* Wasn't that walk through the woods wonderful? But I loved even more our mornings on the lake. *(Going to* c. *to him)*

LAURIE. *(Dreamily)* When we floated under the tower and in the shadows of the old castle.

AMY. With the mountains on every side. *(Both sigh and then look at each other.* LAURIE *is looking down at* AMY *so tenderly that* AMY *is confused and afraid to maintain silence, makes an effort to go on talking, laughing, embarrassed)* How well we used to pull together, didn't we?

LAURIE. *(Stopping short and taking both her hands in his, facing her and looking down at her tenderly, his embarrassment gone, quiet and very earnest)* So well that I wish we might *always* pull in the *same boat.* Will you, Amy? Will you?

AMY. *(Speaking very softly)* Yes, Laurie.

LAURIE. *(Taking her in his arms and kissing her)* When did you begin to care, dear?

AMY. *(Seriously)* Always, I think, Laurie, and I struggled against it, for I thought you loved Jo.

LAURIE. Dear, I was wrong about Jo, and head-strong, and Jo was right. May it be very soon, Amy?

AMY. Yes, dear.

LAURIE. Mrs. Laurence! Oh, I say, how good that sounds!

AMY. *(With curtsey)* My lord——
LAURIE. *(Low bow)* My lady——

*(They embrace. AMY sees MR. LAURENCE over
    LAURIE'S shoulder, gives a scream, picks up
    skirt and runs off R.I.)*

MR. LAURENCE. *(Comes c. stage, smiling, to
where LAURIE is standing, grasps him by both hands,
almost hugging him)* My boy, it's what I've been
hoping for for years.

*(JO and BHAER enter back stage, up L., on platform
    run, pacing to and fro, talking, and not seeing
    the others, backs to audience.)*

LAURIE. I'm glad you're pleased, sir.
MR. LAURENCE. *(Laughing)* What will Jo
say?
LAURIE. *(Who has spied her, pointing across the
bridge and laughing)* Well, I don't think she'll
mind. Oh, I say, Grandpa, get the professor away,
won't you? I want to get the first skim, as we used
to say when we were children and squabbled over
the cream.
MR. LAURENCE. *(Starting across the bridge, up
c. and off on platform)* All right, my lad. *(Half
way across he stops, as if thinking up an excuse,
finally goes over to where the professor and Jo are
talking. LAURIE withdraws to one side, and as soon
as Jo looks his way, beckons her energetically to
come over to him. All this is pantomime)* Professor Bhaer. *(Takes the professor's arm and leads
him off, going L.U.)* Have you seen the Archaeo-
logical Society's last report on the burial customs of
the ancients? *(The professor looks surprised, so
does Jo, and LAURIE is convulsed at the flimsy excuse fabricated by the old gentleman, who links his*

arm through the professor's, and draws him away, evidently against the latter's will, the voices dying away in the distance) I hear it has aroused a storm of protest in Boston. Mr. March and I were discussing it and we wondered if you——

Jo. *(Has, in the meantime, slowly crossed the bridge, comes downstage to* Laurie, *whom she regards suspiciously, evidently expecting trouble or teasing of some kind.* c.*)* What is it, Teddy? You look wicked. Out with it, you bad boy! What mischief have you been up to now?

Laurie. *(*c.*—dropping on his knees and folding his hands as if asking pardon)* Please, ma'am, I'm going to get married.

Jo. Mercy on me, what dreadful thing will you do next?

Laurie. *(Sits back on heels, laughing)* A characteristic, but not exactly complimentary congratulation.

Jo. What can you expect when you take one's breath away and let the cat out of the bag like that? Who is she? Do I know her? Get up, you ridiculous boy, and tell me all about it!

Laurie. *(Springs up lightly)* Yes, you know her, Jo. You've known her longer than I have.

Jo. Miss Randall?

Laurie. No. *(Going* r.*)*

Jo. Not Ned Moffat's sister? Oh, I hope not.

Laurie. Guess again. Come nearer home.

Jo. Not Amy?

Laurie. *(Simply)* Who else could it be, Jo? Haven't you seen?

Jo. Teddy, dear, I am so glad. When did you first find out?

Laurie. I don't just know, but I began to suspect when we were at Valrosa. Such a day! My faith! But wasn't it love among the roses? *(For a moment* LAURIE *forgets* Jo *and goes into a rapturous day dream.* Jo *raises her hands comically, tries to slip away up* C., *but* LAURIE *catches her dress and pulls her back—they laugh)* Jo, dear—*(Pauses, hand on her shoulders)*—I want to say one thing and then we'll put it by forever. I never shall stop loving you, but the love is altered, and I have learned to see that it is better as it is.

Jo. *(Quickly, boyishly)* I tried to show you, Teddy; but you wouldn't listen.

LAURIE. I think it was meant to be and would have come about naturally if I had waited, but I never could be patient and so I got a heartache. Upon my word, I was so tumbled up in my mind at one time that I didn't know which I loved best, you or Amy, and tried to love both alike. *(They laugh)* But when I saw her in the old chateau garden at Valrosa, everything seemed to clear up. You both got into your right places, and I felt sure I could honestly share my heart with sister Jo, and wife Amy, and love them both dearly. Will you believe it, and go back to the happy days when we first knew one another?

Jo. I'll believe it with all my heart—*(Puts hands on* LAURIE'S *shoulders)*—but Teddy, we never can be boy and girl again. We are man and woman now, with sober work to do and we must give up frolicking. We can't be playmates any longer, but we will be brother and sister, to love and help one another all our lives, won't we? *(*Jo *kisses* LAURIE*)*

*(*BHAER *enters again, at back* L. *upper, sees and hears the following.)*

LAURIE. We're going to be married right away. I can't wait. *(Kisses* Jo*)*

*(*BHAER *stops aghast, throws up both hands.)*

Jo. Of course you can't—you always have things your own way.

(Exit both together R.I., talking and laughing, LAU-RIE having tucked Jo's hand under his arm. As they disappear BHAER comes forward. He has a large white sun umbrella under his arm, one of the kind foreigners use, lined with green. As he comes across the bridge he walks deject-edly toward seat R. and drops down on it—looks after them sadly—sighing)

BHAER. Ach, as I feared! There is no place in her heart for an old fellow like me.

Jo. *(Comes backing on, re-entering)* Oh, Mr. Bhaer—*(Pause—bumps into him and sits)*—I was looking for you.

BHAER. *(Rousing himself and trying to look cheerful)* And I for you, Mees Marsche.

Jo. *(Sits beside him, ill at ease, and trying to make conversation)* I was afraid you had gone.

(They do not look at each other. This scene must be played briskly)

BHAER. *(Reproachfully)* Do you believe I should go with no farewell to those who haf been so Heafenly kind to me?

Jo. *(Taking off hat)* No, I didn't, really, but I know you are busy with your own affairs since you came East.

BHAER. I haf hoped to come one time yet before I go.

Jo. You are going, then?

BHAER. *(Sadly, hand on heart)* I haf no longer any beezness here—*it is done!* *(Jo tries to hide her emotion—pause, brushes her tears away—BHAER gets his handkerchief out and mops face)* De sun, he is very hot, Mees Marche—— *(BHAER raises the sun umbrella)* May I not offer you this shade? *(A little pause is broken only by the distant sound of voices and the autumn song of whirring insects and of birds)* Mees Marche, I haf a great favor to ask you. *(Each time his tone suggests a proposal, and then he turns it off)*

JO. *(Looking up expectantly, gladly)* Yes, sir——?

BHAER. *(Hesitatingly)* I am bold to say it, because so short a time remains to me.

JO. Yes, sir——?

BHAER. You remember—the little Tina at Mrs. Kirk's?

JO. *(Dryly)* Oh, yes! The little girl you played menagerie with and who called you her "Effalunt."

BHAER. *(Tenderly)* Yes, my little Tina. She luf to ride on my back. Tina's mother, she is so poor, I wish to get a little dress for my Tina, but I am too stupid to go alone. Will you kindly gif me a word of taste and help?

JO. I'll gladly help you, sir.

BHAER. Ah, das ist aber nicht von einen—— *(Very tenderly—then changes)* Perhaps also a shawl for Tina's mother, she is so very poor and the husband such a care. Yes, a tick, warm shawl would be a friendly ting, you tink so? *(Looks at Jo)*

JO. *(Dryly)* Oh, yes, a very friendly thing.

BHAER. Mees Marche, may we—may we— *(Then quickly)*—go what you call shopping togedder?

JO. I will go shopping with you with pleasure, Professor Bhaer.

(Rises,—she begins picking apples R. of bench and putting them in a basket, rising and stooping at her task. The PROFESSOR sees her, rises quickly, with his umbrella up, stands over her, the um-

*brella bobbing absurdly as he tries to shield her
from the sun; he gives it up and stands* L.C.
sadly. Basket with handle on stage R. *at rise—
also a pile of apples.)*

BHAER. And Mees Marche, dere is something
more I would make so bold as to ask you.

JO. *(*R.*—again expectant—standing up with basket in her hand)* Yes—sir——?

BHAER. May we—may we—make dat shopping
trip to-morrow?

JO. Yes, if you like—— *(Turns* R., *starts picking apples again)*

BHAER. I would like it much. Pardon de haste,
but I haf so little time—— *(Pause)* I haf made
up my mind to go away from here. *(Looking away
—*JO *stoops to pick up apples again—she is crying
and trying to hide her face from* BHAER. *Another
pause.* JO *drops apple, which turns* PROFESSOR *to
her again, taking hold of basket)* May I not take
from you dis burden? *(As he bends he gets a
glimpse of her face—a total change of tone—tenderly)* Heart's dearest, why do you cry?

JO. *(Sobbing)* Because—because—you are going away——

BHAER. *(With a great burst of joy, throwing
basket away up stage* R. Ach, Gott, dot is so good!
*(Gets umbrella back, afraid of himself—in his ex-
citement gesticulating and spreading his arms wide
—umbrella in* L. *hand turned upside down)* Jo, I
have nothing but much lof to give to thee, and I
came to see if thou couldst care for it, and I waited
to be sure that I was something more than a friend.
Am I? Canst thou make a little place in thy heart
for Old Fritz?

JO. Oh, yes! *(She kisses him impulsively—and
he looks at her with all his love in his eyes—they sit
on bench)*

BHAER. Endlich—Endlich! *(Puts up umbrella and they sit behind it. A little silence while they sit behind the umbrella R.I., broken only by fond murmured words, that are half inaudible)* My Jo!

Jo. My Frederick!

(BHAER kisses JO and LAURIE and AMY come R.I. and spy them on seat behind umbrella; they beckon BROOKE and MEG and MR. and MRS. MARCH, who have come strolling in from L. upper on the platform. They all steal down on JO and BHAER. MR. LAURENCE and HANNAH come from L.I., through gate, as they reach positions. LAURIE and AMY start to laugh. BHAER and JO look right at them. BROOKE and MEG take up laugh louder, and then MR. and MRS. MARCH and MR. LAURENCE and HANNAH laugh crescendo until it reaches a shout from all.)

(Positions for Laugh: AMY, LAURIE, JO and BHAER, MEG and JOHN, MR. and MRS. MARCH, MR. LAURENCE, HANNAH. All the action takes place very quickly from now on. PROFESSOR lowers umbrella.)

Jo. Christopher Columbus!

(After general laugh, JO rushes C. MR. MARCH stops her, MR. and MRS. MARCH embrace JO— JO goes R.C.; LAURIE goes to her and hugs her. BHAER goes to R., shakes hands with AMY, MEG and BROOKE. LAURIE and BHAER shake hands. LAURIE goes to back to AMY R., and BHAER joins JO R. of C.)

LAURIE. Hurrah! Hurrah! I knew it—I knew it—I knew it! *(Shakes hands with BHAER)* I told you so four years ago, didn't I, Jo? *(Jo is confused, but too happy to express her feeling.)* Professor,

you've got one girl in a million! Except for mine—
(Going to AMY R., *looking over lovingly at* JO*)*—
her equal isn't on earth.

BHAER. *(*C. *As he tucks* JO's *hands under his
arm)* I know dot, my friend.

LAURIE. What's the plan? Why not a double
wedding?

*(*MR. *and* MRS. MARCH *note this in glad surprise.)*

BHAER. My Jo—ha, ha—that dear funny little
name—— *(Bus. of patting her hand—speaks
quickly)* My Jo and I, we are very simple folk, you
see, and a grand wedding is not for us. My Jo, she
have her heart set on this school, and me to teach
him. I haf a little money, not much, but I tink perhaps it may be done as she wishes.

LAURIE. *(Down* R.*)* Three cheers for the Bhaer-
garden. *(Turns to the others)* Come on, everybody, join hands—and dance around the lovers. *(He
catches* AMY *by the hand and* AMY, MR. LAU-
RENCE'S *hand and they draw the others in as they
dance merrily around* JO *and* BHAER, *singing "Du
Du leigst mir am hertzen"—On second time around
the older ones are breathless.* JO *steps forward,
draws* MR. *and* MRS. MARCH *into the ring, and she
and the* PROFESSOR *join the circle,* MARCH *bends and
kisses his wife.)* What's this? Another pair of
lovers?

JO. Yes, and it's Grandma's birthday.

MARCH. *(Tenderly)* Long life to her and every
happiness.

(Takes MRS. MARCH *in his arms—others all dance
round father and mother, singing "Auld Lang
Syne"—then separate, with apparent uncon-
sciousness into groups;* JO *and* BHAER L. *on one
side of* MRS. MARCH *who has* C. *of stage;* LAU-
RIE *and* AMY R. *corner side of her;* MEG *and*

BROOKE, *together a little at one side;* MARCH
leaning over his wife; MR. LAURENCE *and old*
HANNAH *upstage* L., *looking smilingly on*—MRS.
MARCH *stretches out her hands as if to gather
the whole group into her embrace. She looks
at* MEG *and* BROOKE, LAURIE *and* AMY, JO *and*
BHAER, *her voice trembles with joyful feeling.)*

MRS. MARCH. Oh, my girls! My girls! *(On
this cue start "Auld Lang Syne," very piano, swell
as curtain comes down, playing through calls)* How-
ever long you may live, I can never wish you a
greater happiness than this.

*(Pause—*ROBIN *sings—*MR. MARCH *clasps* MRS.
MARCH'S *hands tenderly—all thinking of* BETH.
*Hold picture for curtain—and the music
swells.)*

MEDIUM CURTAIN

MEG *and* BROOKE   MRS. MARCH *and* MR. MARCH
AMY *and* LAURIE   MR. LAURENCE *and* HANNAH
                    JO *and* BHAER

END OF PLAY

PROPERTY PLOT

ACT I

Ground cloth down for Act 4; faded carpet of old-fashioned, flowered pattern for Acts 1, 2, and 3. Faded damask curtains for both windows, also loops for same.

Lace curtains and brass rods for both windows. One pair of lace curtains and one pair of embroidered curtains for dining room window off R.3, and rods for same.

Bookcases over R. and L.1st doors, and over dining room doors, filled with books.

ON MANTEL R.2.
>One gold clock set at 5 o'clock.
>One small white statue of Venus.
>Two candelabra.
>One match-bowl with sulphur matches.
>One old-fashioned vase.

IN FRONT OF FIREPLACE R.2.
>Andirons.
>Fenders.
>Bellows.
>One brass coal-scuttle.
>One set of fire tools, tongs, poker, stand, all in brass.
>One pair of slippers (Marmee's) placed on fender to warm.
>One red rug.

IN FRONT OF FIREPLACE DOWN STAGE.
>Small green footstool.
>Small cradle with doll.

127

Small upholstered stool.

One work basket, with darning cotton, scissors, needles and stocking (for Beth) darning needles.

Patchwork quilt for doll's cradle.

IN JOG BETWEEN DOORS R.1 AND FIRE-PLACE.

Bookcase with prop books fastened to screen.

IN FRONT OF FIREPLACE UPSTAGE.

One large high-back upholstered armchair.

Manuscript and pencil in same (for Jo).

Small round table, with fruit dish and prop apples, and two real apples in same, with fruit knife.

BAY WINDOW RIGHT-CENTRE.

Four pots of roses on window sill.

Four china saucers under flower pots.

Practical rose in one pot (for Beth).

Cushion seat in bay window covered with old-fashioned cretonne flowered material, covering seat and reaching to floor in front.

Sofa pillows and old-fashioned shawl on seat.

Rag green rug in front.

2 small china figures on window sill L.

Bookcases R. and L. and over bay-window filled with books.

RIGHT OF BAY-WINDOW RIGHT CENTRE

One upholstered chair.

In niche, bust of Plato.

Small vase in niche.

Snow effect in window Right Centre.

LEFT OF BAY-WINDOW RIGHT CENTRE.

Small oblong table.

Modeling clay and tools on same (for Amy).

One upholstered chair.

One bookcase fastened to scene, prop books in same; bust of Shakespeare at right end of top shelf.

Under bookcase one small hanging picture and some of Amy's drawings, fastened to scene.

Piano, old-fashioned cottage piano, with candlesticks, against stairway.   Piano stool.

Crochet mat.

One scarf, one vase with flowers, one writing-case, the old-fashioned writing-box that unfolds, with foolscap paper and quills (for Jo).

Bust of Mozart on piano, also music books and old-fashioned lamp.

One upholstered chair below piano.

What-not, with suitable bric-a-brac.

Small picture under niche above staircase.

UNDER STAIRWAY.

Three-cornered seat in corner under stairway.

Cushion covering seat same as in bay-window, right centre.

Three sofa pillows.

Amy's jacket, hood and mittens (red); Beth's jacket, hood and mittens; Jo's cloak, bonnet and mittens; hanging on rack in closet under stairway.

DESK AT WINDOW L.2.

Seat in window L.2D, with cushions same as in bay-window.

Paper and envelopes inside of desk.

One quill, pad and pencil, foolscap paper, several documents, paper, paper-cutter and one sand-shaker.

Inkwell on top of desk.

One upholstered chair for desk.

One upholstered chair below desk.

Quill pens.

One what-not hanging on scene in jog below desk.

One little old-fashioned teapot and bric-a-brac on same.

One small bookcase made of spools hanging on scene above desk.

TABLE CENTRE (Round mahogany centre table with one centre leg).

One large Bible.

One cloth-bound book for Jo to throw on floor.

One wooden dagger.

One work-basket, thimble, scissors, embroidery and vial in same (for Meg).

One wooden-armed chair L. of table.

One drawing-board in chair left of table, with partly-finished drawing of Venus attached to same, and drawing pencils (for Amy).

Box of drawing pencils.

One upholstered chair back of table.

PROPS OFF STAGE—ACT I

L.I.

Bouquet of flowers (chrysanthemums) for Laurie.

One cardboard, with picture of the Madonna(for Laurie).

Sealed envelope with note enclosed for Meg.

Manuscript paper for Brooke.

Telegram in envelope for Hannah (regular Western Union form, which has not changed).

Two bottles of wine, one flask of brandy, old-fashioned dressing-gown, old-fashioned knit slippers, muffler, for Mr. Laurence.

One roll of paper money (five bills) for Jo.

One roll of paper money (five bills) and a made-out check for Aunt March.

One black crooked-handle cane for Aunt March.

One straight silver or gold-knobbed cane for Mr. Laurence.

One small piece of Jo's hair for Jo.

Snow cloth and door-mat outside of door.

Snow effect on seat outside.

Bag of salt for snow effect for Jo.

ON PLATFORM OFF STAGE UP L.

Crash effect.
One small haircloth trunk.
One small brooch with locks of hair inside, for Beth.
One witch's beard, cloak and hat, for Meg.
Small old-fashioned traveling bag, for Amy.
Paisley shawl and bonnet (Marmee's) for Amy (Wardrobe).
Jo's chapeau, cloak, jacket, boots and one chair.
Sleigh bells for effect off L., also crash effect.

DINING ROOM R.3.

One sideboard, and white cover for same.
One large black tray.
Small tea tray, with cup, saucer, teaspoon and napkin for Meg.
Toasting-fork and five slices of bread on plate for Beth.
Glass bowl with flour for Hannah.
China bowl with cracker crumbs for Jo.
Tumbler with water for Laurie.
One glass vase.
Two candlesticks.

ALL THE ABOVE ON SIDEBOARD

One prop turkey for Hannah.
One triangle for clock strike.
One old-fashioned doorbell for effect.
One white rag rug.

OFF R.1.

Hospital supplies in paper, consisting of bandage cotton, etc., for Marmee.
One red rug, or black-and-white rag rug.
Twelve framed pictures to hang on scene according to numbers.

ACT II—SCENE I

CHANGES

Strike Meg's witch's cloak, wig and beard.

Strike flowers on small table above fireplace and place vase back on mantel R.2.

Strike small candle, toasting fork, plate, bread and slippers.

Place match bowl back on mantel from centre table.

Hang girls' hats, cloaks, etc., in closet under stairway.

Bring glass vase from niche R.3D Right of baywindow, R.C., and place on centre table.

Strike Beth's work-basket to R.1ST.

Strike armchair at fireplace, and bring on small settee in its place.

Bring on Marmee's work-basket, with needle, darning cotton, stockings and china darning-egg, table.

Leave small piece of paper on right side of table for Mr. March to put apple peelings on.

Place Meg's work-basket, with embroidery, on desk L.

Leave apples and fruit knife on small table above fireplace for Mr. March.

OFF STAGE LEFT 1.

Three pink roses.

Spread Eagle newspaper.

One envelope containing checks.

Three stamped envelopes (all for Laurie).

ON PLATFORM 3.

One pair of ice skates for Amy. (Old-fashioned wooden frame skates.)

OFF STAGE R. 1.

One large old Paisley shawl (for Beth).

Jo's writing case, with quills, foolscap paper, etc.

One spool with pins in one end and colored yarn (for Beth).

OFF STAGE R.3.
One milk-pan, with plaster Paris in same, for
Amy's foot.
*Note.—One of Amy's slippers should be molded
into the plaster Paris, with strings attached*

ACT II—SCENE II

Place Meg's workbasket on R. side of table C.
Marmee's basket at back side of table C.
Jo's writing case L. side of table C.
Remove drawing of Venus from Amy's drawing-
board and leave blank sheet of drawing paper
on same.
Bring on four pots of pink flowers for bay-win-
dow R.C.

OFF STAGE L.1.
One volume of Schiller, wrapped up in a copy of
the Spread Eagle, for Bhaer.
Rattle, wrapped in brown paper, for Laurie.
Skein of pink wool wrapped in paper, for Meg.

OFF STAGE R.3.
Crumpled note for Jo.

OFF STAGE R.1.
Old book, Dickens' Pickwick Papers, for Mr.
March.

OFF R.1.
Flower basket for Beth.
*Note.—No change of furniture for this scene.
Take off snow from window R.C. and snow
cloth from outside door, R.1.*

ACT III

CHANGES OF FURNITURE.
    Move centre table about one foot to the left.
    Bring black haircloth sofa on and place in front of bay-window, R.C.
    Place on couch sofa pillows and afghan from window-seat, also Beth's small white pillow.
    Place Jo's writing-case on left of table L.
    Strike settee at fireplace and bring in large armchair in its place.
    Strike sofa pillow in armchair.
    Strike four pots of crysanthemums in window, R.C.
    Bring four pots of roses in place with saucers.

OFF STAGE L.1.
    One broom, one dust-pan, one dust-cloth, for Hannah.
    One bunch of forget-me-nots for Bhaer.

ON MANTEL R.2.
    (New) book of Schiller wrapped in paper with twine, light twine to be broken easily, and three addressed envelopes.
    On small table left of bay-window, Amy's drawing board with picture of Madonna, and drawing pencils.

ON PLATFORM OFF L.3.
    One large pillow with pillow slip (white), with two babies on same, fully dressed. Have cardboard inside of pillow slip to stiffen it.
    One small pillow and covering for babies.
    Two three-cornered blankets for babies' heads.
    Blue and white afghan to cover.
    Pink and blue ribbons on dolls' arms.

OFF R.1.
Beth's work-basket, containing baby jacket, needle,
thread and scissors.
Shawl for Mr. March—old Paisley shawl.
OFF STAGE EFFECTS.
Bird effect of robin, back centre on cue.
Bird effect on cue at end of act, back centre.

ACT IV

Ground cloth.
Grass mats to cover platform.
Flowers and vine for wall.
24 grass mats.
Prop apples on ground R. and some real apples.
Cricket effect on curtain up.
Bird effect on cue.
One large basket filled with prop apples down R.
by tree.
One empty market basket by tree down R.
One bench under tree down R.
Three stacks of prop apples, R.L. and C.
Two mats for runway.
OFF STAGE L.1.
One large lunch basket, for Hannah.
OFF STAGE LEFT 3.
One white umbrella for Bhaer.

CHARACTER TYPES NECESSARY FOR
THE PLAY

JAMES LAURENCE:
A slender, stately, courtly old man, well-dressed
in old-fashioned style; a gentleman of the old
school. Carries a gold or silver-headed walking stick.

MR. MARCH:
  White-haired, scholarly, gentle; his clothes worn, neat and rather clerical in cut; wears spectacles; his voice low, soft, refined.

JOHN BROOKE:
  About 25; brown eyes, good-looking, pleasant, with rather dry humor; unassuming in manner; neatly, simply dressed; appearance that of quiet, kindly, home-loving man.

LAURIE:
  About 18 at opening of play: tall, broad-shouldered, slender, dark, his black eyes and curly hair indicating the Italian; almost a dandy in respect to dress, but wears his clothes unconsciously; charming manners, his boyishness at beginning developing into the attractive, polished man of the world, unspoiled by flattery, with a boyish spirit always; full of fun, with merry smile and wheedlesome ways; rather moody sometimes, but keenly alive to a joke. A born tease.

PROFESSOR FRIEDRICH BHAER:
  About 40. Short, stout, rather thickset, with quantities of turbulent gray-brown hair and a short, shaggy, thick gray beard; wears gray clothes that are mussy, with bulging pockets; speaks with broken German accent; has kindly, benevolent face; type of man one could trust at once and children would adore.

AUNT MARCH:
  Rather stout, elaborately, fussily dressed; little lame from gout; carries long ebony staff tipped with gold, or a crooked cane, on which she leans heavily. She should be richly dressed, hand-

some India shawl, or velvet mantilla, etc. Carries a reticule. Sparkling rings, etc. Everything suggests she denies herself nothing.

MRS. MARCH:

Placid, sweet-faced, rather stout, motherly. Her white hair is worn plain, parted in middle. Plainly, neatly dressed; gentle in manner, adored by everyone. The centre of the March household is Marmee.

HANNAH MULLETT:

Forty, or thereabouts, type of old family servant, faithful and devoted to the Marches. An Irish type. Manner respectful, but masterful; accustomed to rule the March girls and to share in the household joys and sorrows.

MEG:

Eighteen, pretty, plump, fair, with blue eyes and brown hair. Womanly in make-up; industrious, affectionate. Everything about her subdued and restful. Wears silver gray, white, violet, soft pastel shades.

JO:

Seventeen, tall, thin, brown, with decided mouth and eyes, quick, decisive way of speaking. Her hair a beautiful chestnut; legs and arms in the way; awkward, like a colt, in opening act; angular, comical, but not grotesque. Boyish manners; whistles and puts her hands in her apron pockets. A thorough tomboy, but this modifies as play progresses, effect of Beth's illness and death, and the inevitable results of the growing-up and falling-in-love process.

BETH:

Sixteen. Little Tranquility, her entire make-up suggesting the family's pet name for her. A quiet, mouse-like girl, with soft, gentle blue eyes, shy manners. Rosy in first act, with soft

brown hair. She should wear brown with a
touch of red in first act. Always knitting,
sewing or pottering about the plants—never idle.
Shows the effect of illness in second act, and
in third looks white and worn.

AMY:

Fifteen, fair, blue eyes, golden hair, slender, pretty,
decidedly prim in first act. This modifies as
play progresses, until she becomes a graceful,
charming girl in the third. In the fourth, an
attractive, beautiful, cultured woman, with a
genius for dressing and making the most of
herself; well-poised and dignified, with all trace
of self-consciousness gone.

CLOTHES OF CHARACTERS

MR. LAURENCE:

White wig—smooth face—high collar—stock tie
—dark Prince Albert—brocaded vest—shirt ruffles—light trousers—light gaiters. In Act I—
long crocheted woolen scarf—carries ebony
cane with gold or silver head—Should have at
least three changes.

MR. MARCH:

First dress—black trousers—long dark red dressing-gown, rather shabby—stock and black tie—
hair, iron gray and just touching collar—thin,
tall and gentle, with fine features. Second
dress—plain, shabby black frock suit—3d and
4th acts—gray frock suit, with black velvet collar and cuffs.

JOHN BROOKE:

Acts 1st and 2d: Dull brown or green frock coat
—cap—overcoat—soft felt hat—all shabby-look-
ing, but neat—stock collar and tie. 3d act—
frock coat and brocaded vest, little less shabby.
4th act—another change—same style, but better
—straw hat.

LAURIE:
First act: brown trousers and vest—brown short
one—button jacket—brown cap—turn-down collar and dark red Windsor tie—light tan overcoat, rather short. 2d act—light tan suit, short,
boyish style, with brown Windsor tie. 3d act—
gray trousers and blue coat, customary style of
period—with stock—gray felt hat. 4th act—
dark blue or purple suit, with stock collar and
tie—straw hat.

PROFESSOR BHAER:
Second act: Mussy gray suit, with bulging pockets; 3d act—shabby black frock coat with black
velvet collar, flowered vest—stock and tie—old
silk hat—broad, comfortable, unstylish boots or
shoes. 4th act—light linen trousers—brown
frock coat—straw hat—white cotton, green-
lined umbrella, with crooked wooden handle.

AUNT MARCH:
Pink and white make-up—white hair-puffs on side
—carries gold-headed or black, crooked-handle
cane. 1st act—blue, green or purple moire pop-
lin, or watered silk—very full skirt and basque
(no hoops)—very full white petticoat, with three
stiffly starched ruffles. (Note: These petticoats
for all the woman characters.) Over dress she
wears old-fashioned velvet or brocaded plush
dolman—black sash—mere neck scarf with paisley border across the ends—scarf about eight
inches wide and two yards long—small black
bonnet with little purple tips—gloves and a little
silk wrist bag. Old-fashioned jewelry and loud,
old-fashioned earrings, which Meg wears in
last act—also whatever pin or neckchain Aunt
March wears. 2d act—light-colored rich plaid

silk—full skirt and basque—light or white
ground Paisley shawl—small bonnet—small,
old-fashioned quizzing glass on chain or ribbon—cane and bag as in act 1. Under shawl
little black silk cape or wrap, rather be-ruffled.
This shows when she lets shawl fall off in scene
with Meg.

MRS. MARCH:
Act 1—hair parted and rolled over ears—and in
net at back—brown in acts 1, 2 and 3; gray in
act 4. Gray woolen dress and long cloak, circular—plain black bonnet and black cloth bag.
Prunella shoes and red-lined arctic overshoes—
old slippers at fireplace—gray stockings with
tie toes and heels (can be found at almost any
ten-cent store)—small black sateen apron—
white fichu. Paisley shawl and nicer bonnet
for end of act. Act 2, first scene, same. 2d
scene, change to simple, figured gray gown, silk
apron. Act 3, gray and black or purple trimmed
dress—simple and with headdress. Act 4,
purple and black—and bonnet. All dresses a
little better than the rough gray wool of act 1.

HANNAH MULLETT:
Brown sunburned make-up—hair parted and
twisted very tight over ears and into small tight
knot at back. 1st, 2d and 3d acts, dress of brown
Jeans cloth, with different-colored aprons. Act
4, blue and green wash dress, small check or
plaid. No bonnet.

MEG:
First dress: blue, with blue and white striped or
plaid ruffles—hair net—long black cambric
witch's cloak with gold paper trimming—black
peaked hat of same. (Note.—Act 2, scene 2.
Amy wears duplicate of Meg's dress, slightly
altered, but easily recognized as Meg's.) 2d act:

Scene 1, same. Scene 2. buff-colored dress—2 flounces trimmed with coral pink—coral pink hat with white silk scarf around it—pink scarf for shoulders and black shoes, which she changes to pink as she goes out. (Note.—Pink wool for her to wind.) Act 4, golden brown and tan dress trimmed with Persian silk—hair parted and soft around face, with hair net in all sets. White stockings and single-strap slippers.

JO:

Act 1, oxblood red woolen dress, very plain, plain white collar—long chestnut hair in net. Boy's suit—black satin breeches, black velvet jacket, long cloak lined with red, black chapeau with ridiculous cockade—long russet boots. (Note.—Underdress—satin knee breeches for boy's dress—very quick change to be made on platform upstairs.) Heavy-soled button boots, old. Prunella shoes, which she puts on after changing back; no time to button shoes—gray stockings like Mrs. March—gray circular wool cloak with bonnet to match, with embroidered curtain at back of head—brown mittens on black string—short, almost Buster Brown wig, for end of act, also first scene of act 2—same dress. Act 2, scene 2—Green sateen writing apron and cap, with red frills on apron, which has long sleeves and is built to cover her completely—cap has big red bow. Blue and white striped dress and silk Windsor tie. Red dress shoe-top length. Second dress a little longer —last two to the ground. Act 2, scene 2, hair to shoulder when net is off—showing it is growing. Act 3d, tan striped challie or delaine trimmed with brown and brown bonnet trimmed with little red rosebuds. Act 4, lavender figured challie trimmed with apple-green—large leghorn hat trimmed with bow and strings.

BETH:

Acts 1 and 2, dresses to a little below shoetops.
Hair in net. Act 1, brown woolen dress, white
stockings and Prunella shoes—brown knitted
hood with gray wool jacket. Act 2, scene 1,
soft gray dress trimmed with blue; scene 2,
same with coral pink, checked dainty apron
over it. Act 3, pale blue long princess wrapper
trimmed with narrow black velvet, pretty little
lace cape—white wool shoulder shawl—hair
falling on shoulders.

AMY:

Must have golden curls, quite long—very fair
make-up—white stockings. (Note.—If legs are
too "womanly," have her wear red stockings in
first act and scene 1 of second act.) Dress to
calf of leg. Act 1, light gray wool dress
trimmed with scarlet-strap slippers. Act 2,
scene 1—same, but with heavy woolen stockings
over her shoes, brown jacket, pale blue crocheted
hood and bright red mittens on string, when she
goes skating. Act 2, scene 2—Meg's blue dress
of act 1, slightly altered—blue gingham apron
covered with white flour and plaster for first
entrance. Curls slightly tied back—skirts,
ankle-length. Change for end of act to white
silk dress draped in festoons of net caught with
rosebuds. Blue silk scarf for head—carry bouquet of delicate flowers in paper holder. Act
3—green and white challie—hair in net—leghorn hat. Act 4—Rose and figured challie skirt
and waist trimmed with black velvet—pink taf-
feta jacket with pink rose trimmings—white
straw bonnet, trimmed with pink.

Note.—Please follow the colors for the dresses of
the four girls and Mrs. March in Act 1st. This
is necessary.

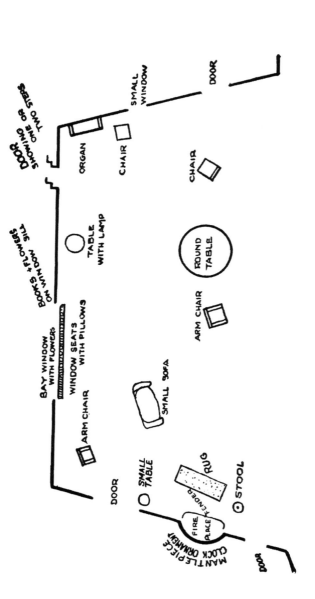

"LITTLE WOMEN" - ACTS 1, 2, AND 3.

SIMPLIFIED STAGE SETTING

MUSIC USE NOTE

Licensees are solely responsible for obtaining formal written permission from copyright owners to use copyrighted music in the performance of this play and are strongly cautioned to do so. If no such permission is obtained by the licensee, then the licensee must use only original music that the licensee owns and controls. Licensees are solely responsible and liable for all music clearances and shall indemnify the copyright owners of the play(s) and their licensing agent, Samuel French, against any costs, expenses, losses and liabilities arising from the use of music by licensees. Please contact the appropriate music licensing authority in your territory for the rights to any incidental music.

IMPORTANT BILLING AND CREDIT REQUIREMENTS

If you have obtained performance rights to this title, please refer to your licensing agreement for important billing and credit requirements.

SAMUEL FRENCH STAFF

Nate Collins
President

Ken Dingledine
Director of Operations,
Vice President

Bruce Lazarus
Executive Director,
General Counsel

Rita Maté
Director of Finance

ACCOUNTING

Lori Thimsen | Director of Licensing Compliance
Nehal Kumar | Senior Accounting Associate
Josephine Messina | Accounts Payable
Helena Mezzina | Royalty Administration
Joe Garner | Royalty Administration
Jessica Zheng | Accounts Receivable
Andy Lian | Accounts Receivable
Zoe Qiu | Accounts Receivable
Charlie Sou | Accounting Associate
Joann Mannello | Orders Administrator

BUSINESS AFFAIRS

Lysna Marzani | Director of Business Affairs
Kathryn McCumber | Business Administrator

CUSTOMER SERVICE AND LICENSING

Brad Lohrenz | Director of Licensing Development
Fred Schnitzer | Business Development Manager
Laura Lindson | Licensing Services Manager
Kim Rogers | Professional Licensing Associate
Matthew Akers | Amateur Licensing Associate
Ashley Byrne | Amateur Licensing Associate
Glenn Halcomb | Amateur Licensing Associate
Derek Hassler | Amateur Licensing Associate
Jennifer Carter | Amateur Licensing Associate
Kelly McCready | Amateur Licensing Associate
Annette Storckman | Amateur Licensing Associate
Chris Lonstrup | Outgoing Information Specialist

EDITORIAL AND PUBLICATIONS

Amy Rose Marsh | Literary Manager
Ben Coleman | Editorial Associate
Gene Sweeney | Graphic Designer
David Geer | Publications Supervisor
Charlyn Brea | Publications Associate
Tyler Mullen | Publications Associate

MARKETING

Abbie Van Nostrand | Director of Corporate
Communications
Ryan Pointer | Marketing Manager
Courtney Kochuba | Marketing Associate

OPERATIONS

Joe Ferreira | Product Development Manager
Casey McLain | Operations Supervisor
Danielle Heckman | Office Coordinator, Reception

SAMUEL FRENCH BOOKSHOP (LOS ANGELES)

Joyce Mehess | Bookstore Manager
Cory DeLair | Bookstore Buyer
Jennifer Palumbo | Customer Service Associate
Sonya Wallace | Bookstore Associate
Tim Coultas | Bookstore Associate
Monté Patterson | Bookstore Associate
Robin Hushbeck | Bookstore Associate
Alfred Contreras | Shipping & Receiving

LONDON OFFICE

Felicity Barks | Rights & Contracts Associate
Steve Blacker | Bookshop Associate
David Bray | Customer Services Associate
Zena Choi | Professional Licensing Associate
Robert Cooke | Assistant Buyer
Stephanie Dawson | Amateur Licensing Associate
Simon Ellison | Retail Sales Manager
Jason Felix | Royalty Administration
Susan Griffiths | Amateur Licensing Associate
Robert Hamilton | Amateur Licensing Associate
Lucy Hume | Publications Manager
Nasir Khan | Management Accountant
Simon Magniti | Royalty Administration
Louise Mappley | Amateur Licensing Associate
James Nicolau | Despatch Associate
Martin Phillips | Librarian
Zubayed Rahman | Despatch Associate
Steve Sanderson | Royalty Administration Supervisor
Douglas Schatz | Acting Executive Director
Roger Sheppard | I.T. Manager
Geoffrey Skinner | Company Accountant
Peter Smith | Amateur Licensing Associate
Garry Spratley | Customer Service Manager
David Webster | UK Operations Director